Y0-CBV-688

I

Crafty Recycling

JEAN LENNANDER ✳ TASSEL PRESS ✳ MINNEAPOLIS, MN

Cover photograph and photograph on page 165 credited to Mark Lynch.

Designed, produced and printed by Bolger Publications/Creative Printing,
3301 Como Ave. SE, Minneapolis, MN 55414

The projects, Shoe Box Basket and Weeping Birch Tree are reprinted by permission from
Popular Handicraft & Hobbies.

All patterns and black and white photographs are by the Author, also color photographs
except as otherwise credited.

Copyright © 1993 by Jean Lennander. Printed and bound in the United States of America.
All rights reserved. No part of this book may be reproduced, or transmitted in any form, or
by any means, without the prior written permission of the publisher. Published by Tassel
Press, Box 6342, Minneapolis, MN 55406. First Edition

Library of Congress Card Number 93-086374
ISBN 0-9639009-1-9

To all the people who contribute

toward making the earth a healthier place to live in.

Acknowledgments

A special thanks to my grandchildren who gave me permission to use their photos, for the enthusiastic encouragment of my children and friends which enabled me to complete this venture.

I want to express my gratitude to Kathy Grey Anderson, whose advice proved helpful in producing quality photos. Also to my husband, for his many, miscellaneous chores.

Preface

Welcome to Crafty Recycling! I hope you will enjoy the exciting craft projects contained in this book.

Based on my twelve years of creating and teaching crafts, I have come up with many fun and useful ideas. The ideas contained in this book developed from the need to find new crafts for my Sunday School class. To save money, I decided to use throwaways and make them into something completely new and different.

I was papering my kitchen at the time and was reminded of the great qualities in wallpaper. Wallpaper is not only durable, nonfading and washable, but it also is available in hundreds of beautiful designs and colors. It was then I decided to create new crafts by camouflaging throwaways with wallpaper.

Novice crafters will be able to achieve a boughten-like appearance to these craft items by following the step-by-step instructions. Novices will also be given guidance as to the best type of wallpaper to use for specific crafts. The directions for each project are complete, except for reference to special methods which are referred to by page or illustration number. Also, many of the items contained in this book can be sold at bazaars or given as gifts.

You may want to gather some throwaway items before you get started. Once you get going, you may not want to stop! Among the recycled materials you will need for these crafts are: vinyl floor covering, plastic bottles, scraps of wood and Masonite, fruitcake tins, cigar boxes, cardboard boxes, tin cans, milk cartons, mat board, and of course, wallpaper.

These days, we all are aware of the importance of recycling. By choosing to create your crafts from throwaways instead of brand new items, you are helping to make this world a cleaner and healthier place.

I know you will find pleasure in creating something new out of something old. Good luck in becoming your own crafty recycler!

General Information

WALLPAPER/WALLCOVERING

There are several types of wallpaper available including, flocked foil, fabric-backed, silk, vinyl and others. The luxurious patterns can enhance tin cans and plastic bottles. If you ask, some wallpaper stores will give you outdated catalogs which are sufficient for small crafts.

There are also discount stores that sell rolls of discontinued patterns. This is an economical source when making several crafts for a specific project.

Some people are allergic to pre-pasted wallpaper. Be aware of this when working with children.

WALLPAPER PASTE

Use wallpaper paste when gluing on cardboard or making large projects. Vinyl wallcovering paste adheres to metal, wood and plastic better than regular wallpaper paste. (Glue adheres before you are able to center the wallpaper.) Also paste is cheaper than glue.

TIN CANS

Wash and remove labels. Use sharp can opener to avoid jagged edges. Sharp edges can be flattened with a pair of pliers.

GLUE

The best glues are those that dry transparently, adhere well, and are water soluble. Some good ones are Sobo and Quik Glue by Delta. Also, Aleene's Tacky Glue works well on all surfaces.

Pour a small amount of glue into a dish for use. Keep main jar covered to prevent thickening. Craft stores sell these types of glue.

DAMP CLOTH

This is a must for every project. Hands and craft must be kept free of glue and paste. Sticky fingers will pull off the paper and you may ruin your craft project.

SCALE MODEL PAINT

Several brands can be purchased at scale model stores and art stores. They are permanent and nontoxic. Dilute with a few drops of water if needed. Stir and pour a small amount into a dish for use. Keep main jar covered to prevent thickening.

BRUSHES

A size 5/0 or 4/0 is ideal for outlining. You can purchase these brushes at scale model stores or art stores. You'll need a 2" brush for pasting large pieces of wallpaper. A watercolor brush is fine for small items.

POSTER BOARD

Can be purchased at drugstores and stores like Target and Kmart. Poster board comes in assorted colors 22" by 28".

FOAM CORE

Used as backing for picture frames. Purchase at picture supply stores and framing stores. It cuts easily with a utility knife, even though it's twice as thick as cardboard.

DRIFTWOOD

Driftwood can be found floating or cast ashore along bodies of water. Driftwood makes interesting hangers for mobiles.

FRAMING

Put frame face down and arrange in order: glass, mat, mounted photos, and corrugated cardboard for backing. Use adaptor in pack to gently push points into frame with putty knife. Pilot holes for oak frame.

MAGNETIC TAPE

It is cheaper to buy magnetic tape by the roll. Cut off as needed. Be sure to round the corners of tape before gluing onto craft. It stays on better and looks neater. It is sold at craft stores.

MOVING EYES

Moving eyes come in various shapes and sizes. Craft stores sell them. Use a toothpick to dab glue on the craft. Gently press eyes on glue.

PATTERNS

Large patterns can be made by outlining inverted platters or bowls. Make small patterns from Cool Whip covers. They last longer and the see-through plastic allows you to center wallpaper images.

JARS/BOTTLES

Choose white or black bottles. They don't need painting and blend with the wallpaper.

The top of a plastic jar must be removed with a utility knife by an adult. Cut below threads where the plastic is softer.

ARTIFICIAL FLOWERS

Wash plastic flowers with Woolite. Dust rayon flowers by taking them outside on a dry, windy day. Craft stores, Target, Kmart, floral shops and Daytons sell them.

ARTIFICIAL FLOWER PARTS

An assortment of artificial flower parts such as stamens, leaves and other greens are sold in variety and craft stores. Stamens are used for antennae on the magnetic butterflies on page 42.

FRAMES

Your frame must have enough depth to accommodate glass, backing and mat. You can buy unpainted frames at large craft and frame stores. Finished frames are sold at photo stores, drugstores and Kmart. Sand and stain the unpainted frames. Dry well. Then, apply tung oil.

SCORE

Always score your cardboard before folding it to get a smoother fold. Draw a light line across the place you want to fold. Hold ruler next to line and draw a dull knife back and forth beside the ruler.

CEILING HOOKS/SCREW EYES

Pilot a small hole before screwing in hooks or screws. This will prevent screws from breaking. You can buy them at Target, lumber yards, builder's supply stores and hardware stores.

SMALL KNOBS

A tiny knob adds a nice finish to the cover of a box. If the bolt is too long, saw it off. Knobs can be purchased at hardware stores, lumber yards and Target.

PICTURE WIRE/HANGER

A wire hanger is the most stable hanger you can buy for your project. Notched hangers are fine for small rounds. Pilot holes 1/3 down from top of frame. Hardware stores and Target sell picture hangers.

GLAZING WITH GLUE

Mix two tablespoons of glue with one tablespoon of water to get the right consistency for glazing. Use glue that dries transparently and is water soluble. Glaze surface of craft and dry overnight.

PLAQUE/ROUND

A round is a 3/4" slice of wood, cut at an angle from a tree limb. They have a rustic quality about them that enhances crafts made with outdoor images such as squirrels or owls. Craft stores sell rounds.

Plaques have a smooth, finished surface. Target, Kmart and craft stores sell plaques.

VINYL FLOOR COVERING

Be sure to use a vinyl floor covering whenever specified. It cuts easily with scrissors. Some floor coverings are brittle, so are not suitable for craft. Check building sites and your attic for leftover pieces of vinyl floor covering.

DRAWING PAPER

Use heavy-duty paper when making a project from catalog wallpaper. It blots out the print on the back of the sample wallpaper. The print is especially bothersome when making lined envelopes. Drugstores, Kmart and art stores sell drawing paper.

SLATS

Slats are used in the May Basket Mobile project. Slats are sold at lumber yards and hardware stores. They come in 8' lengths, 1" wide.

PAINTING BOTTOM OF CANS/BOTTLES

Can: tip upside down over a catsup bottle. Bottle: put a wooden spoon into a can of sand, then tip bottle upside down over handle. Leave until paint is dry.

General Information

CUTOUTS/WINDOWS

In Crafty Recycling, the cutouts in mats for the pictures are sometimes referred to as windows.

WALLPAPER IMAGES

An image is a picture of something in the wallpaper design. Among the crafts using wallpaper images are magnets, party hats and 3-D pencil boxes.

PATTERNS IN BOOK

Trace patterns through onionskin paper, then trace onto plastic or cardboard. A sheet of acetate can also be used. Put over pattern before tracing. Art stores sell acetate in 20" by 24" sheets and also in pads 8-1/2" by 11".

RASP/BEVEL

A rasp is a file used to slope the edges of wood. The rasp was used to bevel top edge of earring tree and pen holder. (See Illustrations 45 and 54.)

PILOT

Pilot is the term used for drilling a slightly smaller hole than screw or nail used to prevent wood from splitting.

Contents

PART ONE ✳ ADULT CRAFT

Contents

PART TWO ✳ CHILDREN'S CRAFT

Contents

PART THREE ❋ SUNDAY SCHOOL CRAFT

PART FOUR ❋ CHRISTMAS DECORATIONS

Adult Craft

Nature and compact designs enhance adult craft projects.

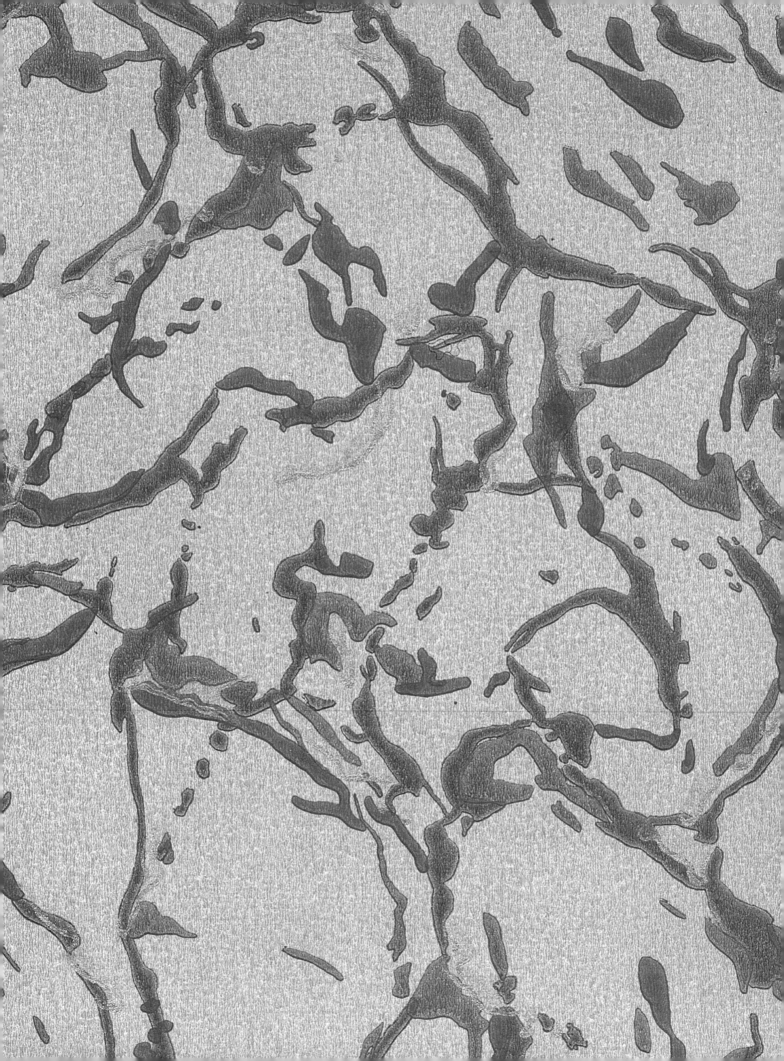

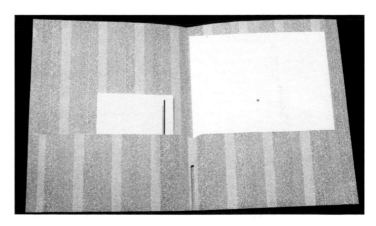

Collage Mat

Illustration 1

MATERIALS FOR COLLAGE MAT

Photos, 11" by 14" frame and glass, poster board 11" by 14" for pattern, vinyl floor covering, white vinyl wallpaper, scissors, glue, yardstick, corrugated cardboard for backing and a damp cloth.

DIRECTIONS FOR COLLAGE MAT

1. Cut a piece each of corrugated cardboard, vinyl wallpaper, vinyl floor covering, and poster board the size of frame.
2. Glue wallpaper to wrong side of floor covering. Wipe firmly with a damp cloth. Dry under weight.
3. Make a poster board pattern to fit your photos. Draw a 1-1/4" border around edge. Pencil in the windows and cut them out.
4. Lay pattern over mat and trace in windows. Cut out windows with a scissors.
5. Next, place mat over cardboard backing and trace in windows. Tape photos on outlines, overlap 1/8".
6. Optional: Paint window edges.
7. Place mat over photos. If needed, adjust photos, then frame.

NOTE

In illustration 2, the top thin cardboard is the pattern for the collage. First, draw a 1-1/4" border around cardboard. Then, trace patterns onto the cardboard to fit your photos. Remember that your windows must be at least 1/8" smaller on all sides than the photos behind them.

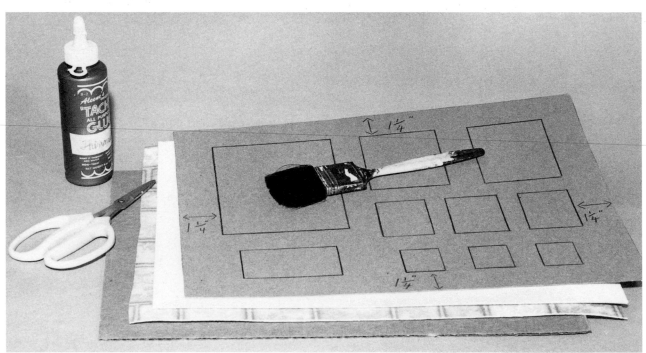

Illustration 2

Rectangle Mat

Oval Mat

Illustration 3

Illustration 4

Frames are 16" by 20". Photos are 11" by 14".
Materials needed for these mats are same as for the
Collage Mat.

Illustration 5

DIRECTIONS FOR RECTANGLE MAT

1. Follow steps 1 and 2 of the Collage Mat.
2. Mark off 3-1/2" on bottom and top, and 3" on the sides. Use a pencil to lightly draw a rectangle shape using these points to form a border.
3. Cut out the rectangle. Center and tape on backing. Place mat over photo and adjust if needed.
4. Paint border around the edge of window with scale model paint. Dry overnight, then frame.

DIRECTIONS FOR OVAL MAT

1. Follow steps 1 and 2 of the Collage Mat.
2. Make a pattern from an inverted oval platter. Center platter and trace onto mat. Cut out.
3. Center and tape photo on backing. Lay mat over photo, adjust if needed.
4. Frame.

Twin Frames

Illustration 6

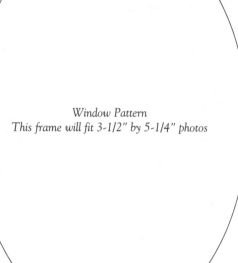

Window Pattern
This frame will fit 3-1/2" by 5-1/4" photos

MATERIALS FOR TWIN FRAMES

Wallpaper, vinyl floor covering, a board 8-1/4" by
12" (3/4" thick), scissors, black scale model paint,
brush for gluing, tablet cardboard, ruler, 5/0 size brush,
glue and damp cloth.

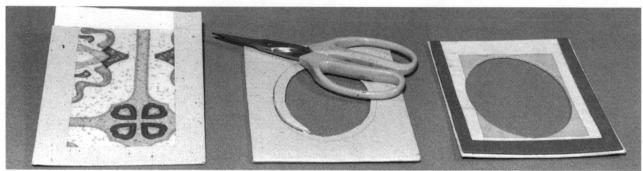

Illustration 7   1.   2.   3.

DIRECTIONS FOR TWIN MATS

1. Cut two pieces of wallpaper 7-1/2" by 6",
   and two of vinyl floor covering 6" by 4-3/4".
   (This will make two mats.)
2. Glue the wallpaper on the wrong side of floor
   covering, overlap on back. (illustration #1)
   Dry under weight.
3. Center pattern on mat, draw and cut out.
   (illustration #2)
4. Paint edge of windows. Let dry.
5. Use mat as pattern to cut out a cardboard edge,
   3/8" on sides and 1/2" on bottom. (illustration #3)
   Glue edge on back of mat. The edge holds photo
   in place. Dry overnight.

DIRECTIONS FOR FRAME BOARD

1. Sand board, then cut a piece of wallpaper
   15-1/2" by 12".
2. Glue wallpaper onto board, snip corners and
   overlap to back. Dry.
3. Spread glue on edging and center mats on board
   1" from top and bottom, and 1-1/4" from sides.
4. Dry under weight. Slide photos in top of mats.
5. Attach hanger.
6. When you are ready to add new photos, tip frame
   upside down.

Horizontal Frame/Vertical Frame

Illustration 8

MATERIALS FOR SMALL FRAMES

Brush, tin shears, plain vinyl wallpaper, cover of a fruitcake tin (for back brace), utility knife, photo, size 5/0 brush for painting window edge, scale model paint, scissors, cardboard and a damp cloth.

NOTE

Use thin cardboard similar to poster board. Patterns for windows and braces are on pages 176.

DIRECTIONS FOR HORIZONTAL FRAME

Same as for Vertical Frame, except increase size of cardboard to 3-3/8" by 4-3/8", and size of wallpaper to 4-3/8" by 5-3/8". Cut a back slit for the brace 1-1/4" from top center.

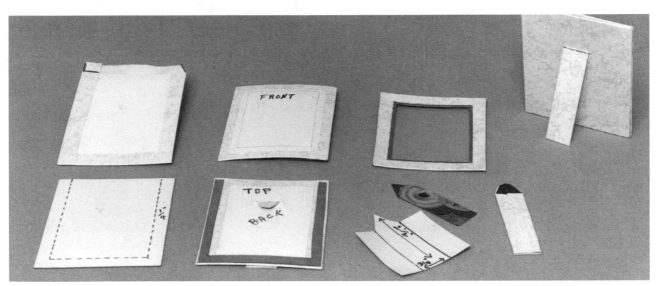

Illustration 9

DIRECTIONS FOR VERTICAL FRAME

1. Cut three pieces of cardboard 3" by 4".
2. Next, cut two pieces of wallpaper 4" by 5", and glue them on two of the cardboards. (for front and back of frame) See illustration 9.
3. Third cardboard: Dot a 1/4" border on three sides. Cut out border and glue inside of back, as photo.
4. Trace window pattern on center of front cardboard. Cut out window and paint around edge. Let dry.
5. Back brace: Cut out back brace and cover with wallpaper. Let dry.
6. Measure down 1-1/2" from top center of back, and cut slit 5/8" wide.
7. Insert brace and bend on dotted line. Pound down with hammer.
8. Apply glue to edging and press on front of frame. Dry overnight.
9. Slide photo in from top.

Daisy Picture

Illustration 10

DIRECTIONS FOR DAISY PICTURE

1. Press daisies in telephone book between paper towels until dry.
2. Cut out a bright piece of wallpaper the size of frame.
3. Tape to cardboard backing.
4. Use a toothpick to gently glue the daisies to the wallpaper. Dry.
5. Frame and attach hanger.

Illustration 12

Framed Keepsake

Illustration 11

MATERIALS FOR FRAMED KEEPSAKE

An 8" by 10" frame, glass, and corrugated cardboard, scissors, leaves, silk wallpaper, brush, toothpicks, card, paper punch and damp cloth.

DIRECTIONS FOR FRAMED KEEPSAKE

1. Press leaves between paper towels in a telephone book until dry.
2. Cut an 8" by 10" piece each of silk wallpaper and cardboard. (The cardboard is for the backing.)
3. Center card on cardboard backing and tape in place.
4. Make a frame for the card from the silk wallpaper. Put over card.
5. Prepare the flowers by removing stem and centers. Glue two flowers together. Press flat and let dry.
6. Use a toothpick to gently glue leaves around frame. Then glue on the flowers.
7. Punch out black wallpaper centers and glue on flowers. Let dry.
8. Frame and attach hanger.

NOTE

Use a damp cloth to press on glued flowers to prevent them from sticking to your fingers.

Stained Plaque

Illustration 13

White Plaque

Illustration 14

MATERIALS FOR WHITE PLAQUE

Large plaque, silk pink roses, scissors, light pink wallpaper, glue, white enamel paint, white ribbon, hanger, thin wire and a damp cloth.

DIRECTIONS FOR WHITE PLAQUE

1. Paint plaque and dry overnight.
2. Put flowers on plaque and mark spot where you want them secured. Drill two holes with a 1/16" drill. (Secure in two places if needed.)
3. Place plaque face down on the wrong side of wallpaper. Trace and cut out. Then trim off 3/4" around edge so that plaque will show.
4. Glue wallpaper on plaque. Dry.
5. Attach hanger.
6. Poke wire through wallpaper and over flower stems through other hole to back. Twist wires tightly.
7. Run ribbon under stems and tie bow.

DIRECTIONS FOR STAINED PLAQUE

1. Smooth plaque with a fine grade of sandpaper.
2. Stain plaque and dry overnight.
3. Lay flowers on plaque and mark where you want flowers secured.
4. Drill two holes 3/8" apart with a 1/16" drill.
5. Choose a subtle flowered wallpaper matching the flowers.
6. Then follow steps 3 through 7 of White Plaque.

NOTE

Use plastic coated electric wire if available. It is used in wiring large appliances. Refer to illustration 17 to see how wire is secured in back of plaque.

Weeping Birch Tree

Owl Plaque

Illustration 15

Illustration 16

DIRECTIONS FOR OWL PLAQUE

1. Use a round with lots of bark.
2. Apply tung oil to seal wood and make it look smooth.
3. Use image of an owl, squirrel, bird, or raccoon.
4. Trim image and glue to plaque.
5. Attach hanger. Glue on eyes.

INFORMATION FOR WEEPING BIRCH

Peel off loose bark from a birch tree. Take only what you will need because it curls after it dries. A 3-D effect is achieved by gluing only the center of leaves. Use a few bark scars and lay lines horizontal so tree will appear realistic.

MATERIALS FOR WEEPING BIRCH TREE

Scissors, waterbased paint, vinyl wallpaper, corrugated cardboard, black felt-tipped pen, birch bark, frame and glass, glue, damp cloth, utility knife and vinyl wallpaper in colors of fall leaves.

DIRECTIONS FOR WEEPING BIRCH TREE

1. Cut a piece of corrugated cardboard, the size of your frame. The frame at left is 20" by 30".
2. Paint sky and grass. Let dry.
3. Sketch trunk and branches.
4. Glue on bark, overlapping occasionally. Then outline bark with a black, felt-tipped pen.
5. Cut out leaves from wallpaper using your own pattern. To brighten picture, use green, orange and red colors. (it is easier to cut three at once.)
6. Use a small brush and glue only the center of leaves.
7. Dry overnight, then frame.

Bird Round

Illustration 17

Illustration 19

MATERIALS FOR BIRD ROUND

Berries and seeds, round, white wallpaper, glue, wire and scissors.

DIRECTIONS FOR BIRD ROUND

1. Place round, face down on wrong side of wallpaper and trace.
2. Trim off 3/4" of this wallpaper and glue to center of the round.
3. Mark spot where you want to secure stems. Drill two holes, using a 1/16" drill.
4. Place berries on plaque. Thread wire through right hole and around stems, back through other hole.
5. Twist wires tightly and trim.
6. Secure bird to stems with wire attached to bird.

Butterfly Round

MATERIALS FOR BUTTERFLY ROUND

Seed stems, bright wallpaper, magnetic butterfly, scissors, hanger, round and glue.

DIRECTIONS FOR BUTTERFLY ROUND

1. Follow steps 1 and 2 of Bird Round.
2. Attach hanger to back of round.
3. Glue seed stems to plaque, then glue a tiny piece of magnetic tape in the middle of stems. Let dry.
4. Place a magnetic buttefly over magnet. (Directions for butterfly are on page 42.)

Illustration 18

Key Rack

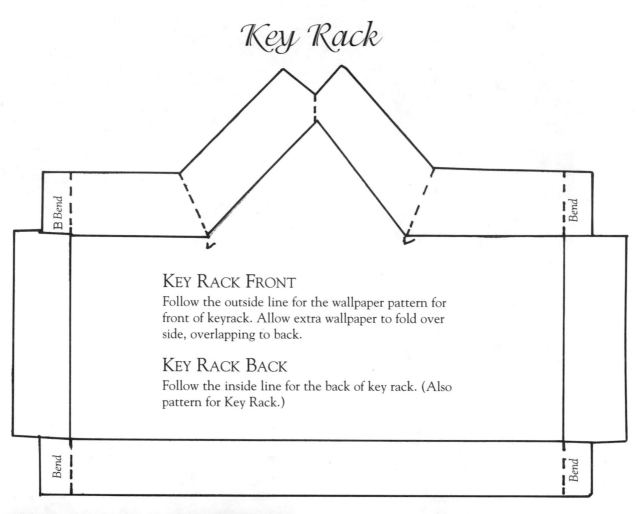

KEY RACK FRONT

Follow the outside line for the wallpaper pattern for front of keyrack. Allow extra wallpaper to fold over side, overlapping to back.

KEY RACK BACK

Follow the inside line for the back of key rack. (Also pattern for Key Rack.)

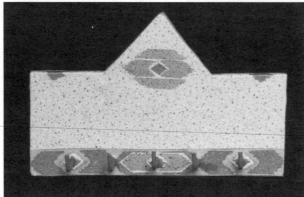

Illustration 20

MATERIAL FOR KEY RACK

Wallpaper, five square-bend screw hooks, 1/4" Masonite board, glue and brush.

DIRECTIONS FOR KEY RACK

1. Draw pattern in corner of board so you only have to saw two sides.
2. Sand if necessary.
3. Trace pattern for the front on the right side of wallpaper. Cut on dotted lines and apply glue.
4. Center smooth side of key rack on wallpaper. Bend over tabs, then the ends.
5. Glue down top and bottom overlap.
6. Draw pattern for back of rack.
7. Glue on back. Next, glue on a border for bottom of key rack.
8. Pilot holes on bottom about 3/4" apart.
9. Attach hanger.
10. Twist in hooks.

NOTE

When finished, glue a tiny strip of wallpaper over space at ✔ mark.

Purse Clipboard

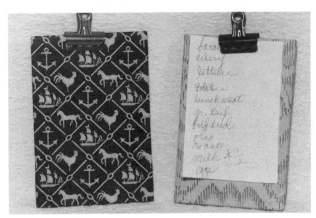

Illustration 21

Lap Clipboard

Illustration 23

MATERIALS FOR CLIPBOARDS

Wallpaper, Masonite board, brush, clips, glue, ruler and scissors.

DIRECTIONS FOR PURSE CLIPBOARD

1. Cut a 3/16" thick piece of Masonite board 3-5/8" by 5-1/2".
2. Then, cut a piece of wallpaper for front of board 4-3/4" by 6-1/2".
3. Put glue on paper. Center board on it and overlap sides to back.
4. Cut off excess paper and overlap ends.
5. Glue paper on back. Add clip as shown in illustration 21.

DIRECTIONS FOR LAP CLIPBOARD

1. Cut a 9-1/2" by 12" piece from a 3/16" thick plywood. Sand smooth.
2. Cut a piece of wallpaper 10-5/8" by 13" for front of board.
3. Apply glue to paper and center board on it. Overlap ends and cut off excess paper, then do sides.
4. Glue piece on back, the size of board. Attach clip as shown in illustration 23.

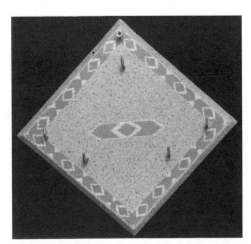

Illustration 22

Belt Rack

DIRECTIONS FOR BELT RACK

1. Saw a piece of pine 7-1/2" by 7-1/2", 3/4" thick. Rasp top edge. (Refer to illustration 45.)
2. Cut a piece of wallpaper 10" by 10". Apply glue to wallpaper. Center board face down. Overlap sides to back. Snip off excess paper and fold over other sides.
3. Glue on trim.
4. Pilot holes and screw in hooks.

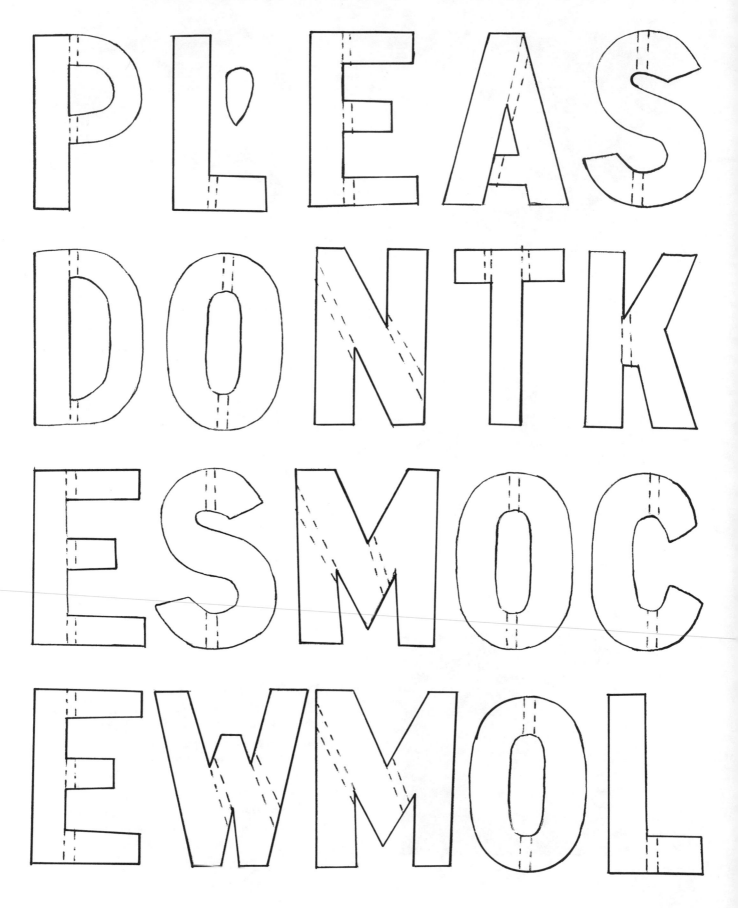

Welcome Sign

Illustration 24

MATERIALS FOR WELCOME SIGN

Ruler, wallpaper, magnetic tape, 1/8" thick Masonite board, flower stamens for butterfly antennae, magnetic butterflies, glue and damp cloth.

DIRECTIONS FOR WELCOME SIGN

1. Cut a piece of Masonite 7" by 11-1/4" and sand edges smooth.
2. Cut out wallpaper trim 1/2" wide, and glue on smooth side of board, 1/2" from edge.
3. Cut out letters, then glue to board as shown in illustration 24.
4. Glue tiny strips of magnetic tape on board for butterflies.

Small Magnet Butterfly

Body and Butterfly Pattern

DIRECTIONS FOR SMALL BUTTERFLY

1. Glue two small pieces of pattern wallpaper, back-to-back. Dry overnight under weight.
2. Cut out three butterflies and six single, black bodies.
3. Glue one on top of each butterfly. (See illustration 93.)
4. Shorten two stamens and glue on back of butterfly head, then glue other body over antennae and press together.
5. Glue strip of magnetic tape on back of body. Dry, then put butterfly on top of magnet on board.
6. Complete two more butterflies.

NOTE

Cut out six black bodies, one for front and one for back of butterfly. When finished, cut butterfly wings on dotted lines and lift up wings gently.

Illustration 25

Don't Smoke Sign

MATERIALS FOR DON'T SMOKE SIGN

1/8" thick Masonite board, glue, ruler, wallpaper, brush and damp cloth.

DIRECTIONS FOR DON'T SMOKE SIGN

1. Cut a piece of Masonite 7-3/4" by 11-1/4" and sand edges smooth.
2. Cut out a piece of wallpaper 9" by 12-3/4" and glue to smooth side of board. Snip corners and overlap to back.
3. Cut a 1/4" trim and glue around edge of board.
4. Cut out letters. If you want a stenciled look, cut out on dotted lines.

Illustration 26

MATERIALS FOR DOUBLE FLOWERS

Stem wire, wallpaper, brush, green floral tape, chenille stems or wire with attached centers, azalea calyxes, scissors and a damp cloth.

DIRECTIONS FOR DOUBLE FLOWERS

1. Glue wallpaper back-to-back and dry overnight under weight.
2. For each flower, cut two of the small patterns and two of the large patterns. Use a small paper punch to punch hole in center of flowers.
3. Cut a piece of chenille stem, 2-1/2" long and roll a ball at one end.
4. Take two large flowers and put two small flowers on top. Push the chenille center through top of flowers.
5. Hold stem wire tightly under flower and twist chenille firmly around wire. (See illustration 27.)
6. Push up the calyxe, tight under flower, then begin wrapping an 8" piece of floral tape around wire, winding in the leaves as you go. Vary length of stems.
7. Bend bottom petals down and the other three flowers up. This gives flower double effect.

NOTE

You can use either the stem attached to center or make a center from a 2-1/2" piece of chenille stem. Twist a ball, then push down through hole of flower and wrap around wire. (See illustration 27.)

Cut two

Cut two

Illustration 27

Directions for Peanut Butter Vase

1. Mark a cutting line on jar with a felt-tipped pen. (Notice cutting line in illustration 29.)
2. Cut off top of jar with utility knife. Even off with scissors, then sand smooth.
3. Paint top edge and jar bottom with gold paint. (See illustration 29.) Dry overnight.
4. Cut wallpaper for vase from pattern on page 176.
5. Glue wallpaper on vase. Press out air bubbles with damp cloth.
6. Fill vase 3/4 full of sand. Place flowers in vase.

Note

In illustration 29, the middle jar is a Peter Pan peanut butter jar. Top threads are too hard to cut, so cut top

Illustration 29

of jar off, further down with a utility knife. See cutting line as shown.

Painted Daisies

Illustration 28

Directions for Painted Daisy

Same as for the Double Flowers but cut two daisies. Turn top flower so the petals alternate with the bottom flower. Leave flower flat.

Directions for Heart Flowers

1. Follow steps 1-7 of the Double Flowers but trace only one flower pattern for each flower.
2. Make tiny hearts from red wallpaper and glue on flower petals as shown in illustration 30.

Note

Use gold paint out of doors or in a well-ventilated room.

Heart Flower

Illustration 30

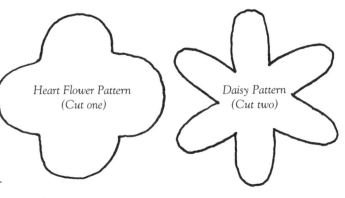

Heart Flower Pattern (Cut one)

Daisy Pattern (Cut two)

Cetaphil Vase

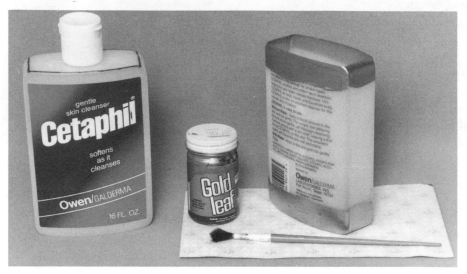

Illustration 31

MATERIALS FOR CETAPHIL VASE

Wallpaper, black felt-tipped pen, glue, gold paint and small brush, ruler, scissors, gluing brush, sandpaper, Cetaphil or Nutraderm bottle and a damp cloth.

DIRECTIONS FOR CETAPHIL VASE

1. Mark a cutting line above slope on top of bottle. (See illustration 31.)
2. Using a pointed scissors, jab a hole near the cap and cut out the cap.
3. Then, trim off to cutting line and sand smooth.
4. Soak bottle in warm suds to remove front label. Dry well.
5. Paint the top edge and bottom of bottle with gold paint as shown in illustration 31. Dry overnight.
6. Cut a piece of wallpaper 5" by 10" and glue on bottle. Let dry.
7. Fill 3/4 full of sand, then place flowers in vase.

NOTE

Coordinate the color of vase with your flowers. A color like a white marble look would go nicely with the gold edges and with any color flower.

Illustration 32

Nature Pen Holders

Illustration 33

Illustration 35

These pen holders can be made from any soft, large, plastic container. Try an empty cinnamon container or shampoo bottle. Remember to choose wallpaper that might interest the person using it. (You may want to use wallpaper that reminds them of their hobbies.)

MATERIALS FOR PEN HOLDERS

Utility knife, felt-tipped pen, scissors, gold paint, brush, sandpaper, ruler, glue, 2" diameter plastic can and wallpaper with nature images.

DIRECTIONS FOR NATURE PEN HOLDERS

1. Remove paper from container and mark a line 3" from bottom.
2. Cut on line with utility knife.
3. Even off line with scissors and sand edge smooth.
4. Paint top and bottom edges with gold paint. (Do your painting outdoors.)
5. Cut two pieces of wallpaper 2-1/2" by 7-1/4". Glue on outside and inside of can.

Illustration 34

Desk Set

NOTE

The pen holder and matching small frame is a nice Father's Day gift. (Follow directions for small frames on page 5.)

Tall Pen Holder/Photo Bookmark

Illustration 36

DIRECTIONS FOR PHOTO BOOKMARK

1. Draw a bookmark 1-1/4" by 5" from thin cardboard. Round off the top corners.
2. Paint edges on front side with gold paint. When dry, turn it over and paint edges on other side.
3. Cut out two more bookmarks 4-7/8" by 1". (Use wallpaper that matches pen holder.)
4. On one of these bookmarks, draw an oval pattern for photo window, and cut it out.
5. Optional: After step 4, paint a border around window. Dry well.
6. Place photo on top center of bookmark, then put wallpaper frame over photo. Adjust photo, and when centered, draw line around photo.
7. Glue photo on line. Then, glue the wallpaper frame on top.
8. Glue on wallpaper back.
9. Place between paper towels and dry under weight overnight.

In illustration 36, the ducks on bookmark were cut out from wallpaper, then glued on to match holder.

MATERIALS FOR TALL PEN HOLDER

Ruler, shampoo bottle, wallpaper, sandpaper, gold paint, damp cloth, small brush and a separate brush for gluing.

DIRECTIONS FOR TALL PEN HOLDER

1. Cut off shampoo bottle to 4-1/4". Sand smooth.
2. Paint bottom and top edges with gold paint. (Paint it outdoors.)
3. Glue wallpaper inside and outside of holder. (Allow for 1/4" of gold edging on top and bottom.)

MATERIALS FOR PHOTO BOOKMARK

Thin cardboard, scale model paint, ruler, gold paint, wallpaper, photo, scissors, brush and glue.

Small Paintbrush Can

DIRECTIONS FOR PAINTBRUSH CAN

Same as for the Tall Pen Holder but cut bottle off at 5".

Illustration 37

3-D Pencil Holder

Tin Pencil Can/ Comb Holder

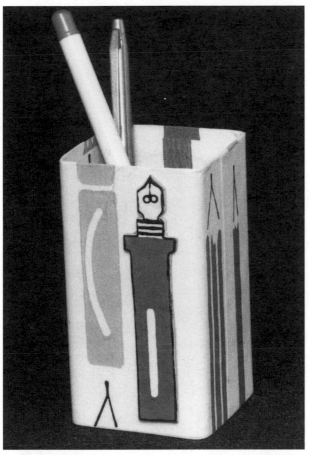

Illustration 38

Illustration 39

MATERIALS FOR 3-D PENCIL HOLDER

2" square can, brush, glue, ruler, scissors, vinyl floor covering, an image from same wallpaper used for holder and damp cloth.

DIRECTIONS FOR 3-D PENCIL HOLDER

1. Cut can to height of 4".
2. Cut a piece of wallpaper 4-1/2" by 8-3/4". Glue on outside of can. Cut corners at top and overlap inside.
3. Cut another piece 3-1/2" by 8-1/2" and glue inside of can.
4. Glue image to the wrong side of floor covering. Dry overnight under weight.
5. Cut out image and glue to front of can. Leave flat until dry.

NOTE

A round plastic bottle can be used for holder by adjusting wallpaper measurement.

MATERIALS FOR TIN PENCIL CAN

Damp cloth, scissors, 5-1/2 oz. juice can, wallpaper with a black background, black spray paint and glue.

DIRECTIONS FOR TIN PENCIL CAN

1. Spray paint can black. Let dry.
2. Cut a strip of wallpaper 3-5/8" by 7-1/4".
3. Apply glue to wallpaper and glue to outside of can. Press down with a damp cloth.

MATERIALS FOR COMB HOLDER

Wallpaper with black background, utility knife, black spray paint, ruler, a 2-1/2" diameter plastic bottle, glue, scissors and damp cloth.

DIRECTIONS FOR COMB HOLDER

1. Cut bottle to 5-1/4" high.
2. Spray paint can. Dry well.
3. Cut a piece of wallpaper 4-3/4" by 9". Glue on bottle. Leave a black margin on top and bottom.

Spindle/Pencil Can

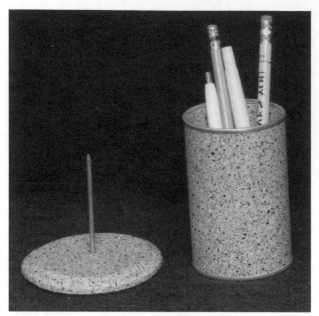

Illustration 40

The baking powder can is ideal because the edge matches the aluminum nail perfectly. Cut out inside edge in can with a can opener.

MATERIALS FOR PENCIL CAN

Wallpaper, scissors, damp cloth, Calumet baking powder can, glue, brush for gluing and ruler.

DIRECTIONS FOR PENCIL CAN

1. Cut two pieces of vinyl wallpaper 3-5/8" by 8". Glue them on inside and outside of can.

MATERIALS FOR SPINDLE

Glue, wallpaper, aluminum 3" nail, scissors, 3-1/2" plaque and felt for bottom of spindle.

DIRECTIONS FOR SPINDLE

1. Pilot a small hole through the center of plaque. Drive the nail through the hole.
2. Tear wallpaper into strips and glue on spindle in pieces. See illustration 62 and 63.

Carpenter's Pencil Box

MATERIALS FOR CARPENTER'S PENCIL BOX

Half-and-half carton, wallpaper, damp cloth, vinyl floor covering, black scale model paint, a size 5/0 brush, scissors and brush for gluing.

DIRECTIONS FOR CARPENTER'S PENCIL BOX

1. Cut off top of carton to 3-3/4"
2. Cut a piece of wallpaper 3-1/2" by 3-1/2" and glue on bottom. Snip corners and overlap to sides.
3. Next, glue a piece of wallpaper 4-1/4" by 12" on outside of box. Snip corners and overlap to inside.
4. Cut a piece of wallpaper 3-3/4" by 12" and glue inside of box.
5. Cut a square 2-3/4" by 2-3/4" for inside bottom of carton.
6. Glue a piece of wallpaper 4" by 8" onto wrong side of vinyl floor covering. Dry under weight.
7. Trace four sets of geometric shapes onto the wallpaper. (Patterns are on page 175.)
8. Outline shapes with black paint. Let dry. Glue a set on each side.

Illustration 41

9. Follow directions on page 50 to make pencil holder, except shorten length to 2-3/4".

Pencil Block/Tier Pencil Block

Illustration 42

MATERIALS FOR PENCIL BLOCK
Wallpaper with a wood finish design, a finished 4 by 4, damp cloth, glue, scissors and 5/16" spade bit.

DIRECTIONS FOR PENCIL BLOCK
1. Cut a 3-1/2" piece from a finished 4 by 4. Drill nine holes 2" deep with a 5/16" spade bit.
2. Cut a piece of wallpaper 4-1/2" by 4-1/2". Glue over holes, overlapping evenly on all sides. (See below.)
3. Then, cut a piece of wallpaper 3-1/2" by 15" and glue around block.
4. Dry overnight. Use X-acto knife to cut out holess.

Illustration 43

Tier Pencil Box

MATERIALS FOR TIER PENCIL BOX
Ruler, half-and-half carton, wallpaper, 5/16" spade bit, block of wood 2-3/4" by 2-5/8" (2-1/2" high), scissors, vinyl floor covering and glue.

DIRECTIONS FOR TIER PENCIL BOX
1. Cut the half-and-half carton 3-3/4" high.
2. Cut a piece of wallpaper 4-1/2" by 12" and glue on outside. It allows for overlap on top and bottom.
3. Glue a piece 3-1/2" by 11-3/4" inside.
4. Glue an image on back side of floor covering. Dry overnight. Cut out and glue on front of box.
5. Cut a piece out of the block of wood. (See illustration 42.)
6. Drill in holes with a 5/16" spade bit. Sand and check fit in box.
7. Glue a strip of wallpaper 7" by 4-1/2" over holes. Begin at top. It is not necessary to cover sides.
8. Dry overnight. Use X-acto knife to cut out holes. Put in box.

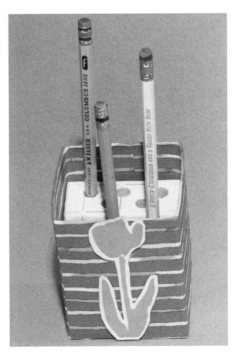

Illustration 44

Desk Accessory

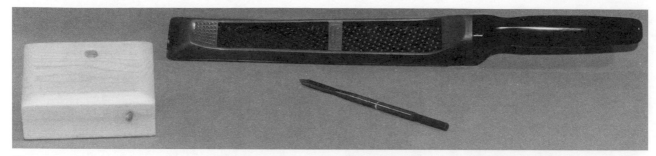

Illustration 45

Above block of wood is a finished 2 by 4, 3-7/8" long. (1-1/2" by 3-1/2")

Illustration 46

MATERIALS FOR DESK ACCESSORY

Ruler, a finished 2 by 4, 3-7/8" long, felt, glue, scissors, wallpaper, a 3/8" spade bit and a damp cloth.

DIRECTIONS FOR DESK ACCESSORY

1. Bevel 1/4" around edge of block with a rasp. Sand smooth.
2. Use a 3/8" spade bit to drill a hole at a 45° angle, 1-1/2" deep, 1" from top edge.
3. Cut a piece of wallpaper 4-1/4" by 4-3/4".
4. Center and glue on top of wood. Snip edges of wallpaper and overlap on all sides.
5. Cut two pieces of wallpaper 1-1/2" by 4-1/2" for long sides. This allows for overlap on sides and bottom.
6. Then, cut two pieces 1-1/2" by 3-3/8" and glue on ends. (Overlap on bottom only.)
7. Glue a piece of felt on bottom.
8. Cut out hole with X-acto knife.

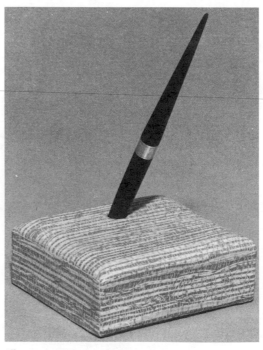

Illustration 47

Tissue Rack

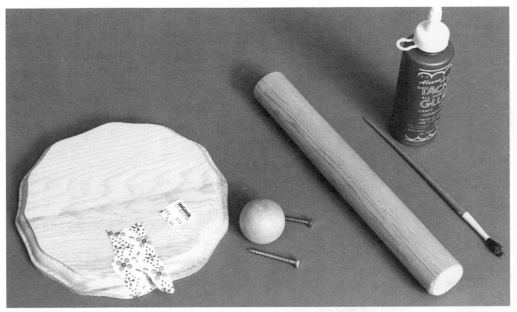

Illustration 48

MATERIALS FOR TISSUE RACK

Ruler, a 7" round plaque, 10" long piece of closet pole, round drawer knob with 1" base, glue, wallpaper, one 1-1/2" screw, brush and felt.

DIRECTIONS FOR TISSUE RACK

1. Round off top end of pole so it will fit knob.
2. Tear thin strips of wallpaper and glue to plaque and knob. (Turn to illustrations 62 and 63 to see how to tear wallpaper.)
3. Next, cut a piece of wallpaper for pole 9-1/2" by 5" and glue onto pole. Dry overnight.
4. Attach knob to pole with a 1-1/2" wood screw. (Screw comes with knob.)
5. Pilot hole in bottom of plaque. Attach pole to plaque with screw.
6. Glue felt to bottom of plaque.
7. Glaze Tissue Rack by Applying a thin coat of thinned glue to surface.

Illustration 49

Round Necklace Tree

Illustration 50

MATERIALS FOR NECKLACE TREE

Glue, 1" dowel, 3-1/2" plaque for base of tree, eight cup hooks, 1-1/2" wood screw, glue, brush, felt for bottom of tree, damp cloth and miniature pattern wallpaper.

DIRECTIONS FOR NECKLACE TREE

1. Cover base with wallpaper by tearing thin strips and gluing on, piece by piece, overlapping edge.
2. Wipe off surface glue with damp cloth as you go.
3. When finished, press down wallpaper again with damp cloth, especially on all ridges.
4. Now, tear paper and glue to top of pole the same way.
5. Cut a 10-1/2" piece from the dowel.
6. Measure a piece of wallpaper 10-1/2" by 5-1/4" and glue around pole.
7. Pilot hole in bottom center of base and attach to pole.
8. Pilot holes with nail, 1/2" from top edge, 1/4" apart. Then, screw in hooks.
9. Glaze tree with thinned glue.
10. Dry overnight and glue felt on bottom of base.

NOTE

For instructions on how to tear wallpaper, see illustrations 62 and 63 on page 29.

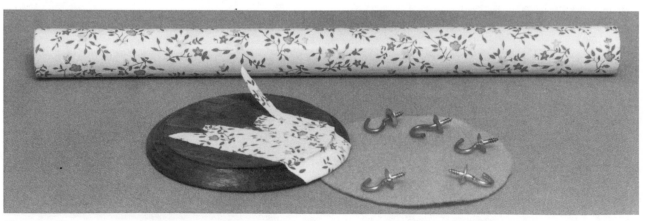

Illustration 51

Square Base Tree

Wall Necklace Tree

Illustration 52

Base of tree is 2-3/4" by 2-3/4".

DIRECTIONS FOR SQUARE BASE TREE

1. Cut a 10-1/2" piece from a 1" dowel. Smooth ends with sandpaper.
2. Glue a piece of wallpaper 10-1/2" by 5-1/4" around pole. Then, glue a 1" circle on top of pole.
3. Cover base with a piece of wallpaper 5-1/8" by 5-1/8".
4. Center, and glue top down. Cut corners at an angle so they butt together like a picture frame.
5. Press down second tier, overlapping to back.
6. Follow step 7-10 of Round Necklace Tree to complete tree.

MATERIALS FOR WALL NECKLACE TREE

A board 14" by 8" (5/8" thick), glue, scissors, yardstick, wallpaper, seven large cup screws, wire, and two eyescrews for hanger.

DIRECTIONS FOR WALL NECKLACE TREE

1. Smooth edges with sandpaper.
2. Cut a piece of wallpaper 10" by 16".
3. Apply glue and center wallpaper on board. Press surface firmly, snip corners and overlap to back.
4. Next, cut wallpaper for back 7-3/4" by 13-3/4" and glue on.
5. Cut another piece of wallpaper 1" by 10" and glue across top for trim.
6. Pilot holes in center of trim and screw in cup hooks.
7. Attach hanger to back.

NOTE

If you have left-over wallpaper from wall, use that for Wall Tree. It would blend nicely.

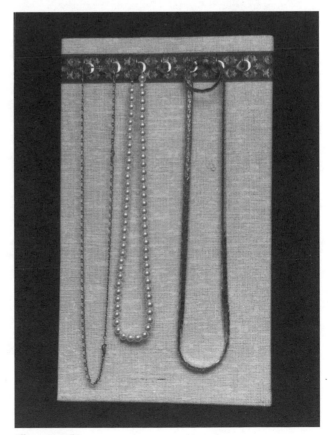

Illustration 53

Pierced Earring Tree

Illustration 54

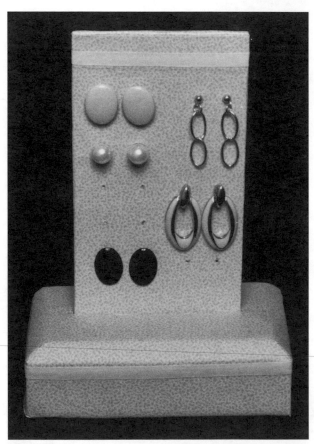

Illustration 55

MATERIALS FOR BASE OF TREE

Piece of finished 2 by 4 (1-1/2" by 3-1/2"), 1/8" thick cardboard, glue, rasp, damp cloth, 1/16" drill, scissors, brush, wallpaper and ruler.

DIRECTIONS FOR THE BASE OF TREE

1. Cut a finished 2 by 4, 5" long.
2. Bevel 1/4" around top edge with a rasp. Sand edges smooth.
3. Center a line 3-3/8" long on top of base.
4. Use a 1/8" router bit to mill out a groove on line to depth of 3-3/16".

DIRECTIONS FOR EARRING TREE

1. Cut a piece of cardboard 3-3/8" by 5-7/8" (1/8" thick).
2. Cut a piece of wallpaper 3-3/8" by 1-1/2". Glue over top of cardboard.
3. Cut a piece of wallpaper 5-7/8" by 7-3/4". Glue around cardboard. (See illustration 54.)
4. Cut a piece of wallpaper 4-1/2" by 6-3/8" and glue on top of base. Snip corners so they meet like a picture frame. Dry overnight.
5. Next, cut a piece of wallpaper 1" by 18" and glue around sides of base.
6. Drill post holes through cardboard, using a 1/16" drill.
7. Cut slit in wallpaper on base and dribble glue in groove. Press in cardboard.
8. Glue a piece of felt 3-1/8" by 5" on bottom of base.
9. *Trim:* Glue a 1/4" strip of wallpaper 1/4" from top and around edge of base. Choose a darker shade in the same color as tree.

NOTE

Cardboard used for tree must be 1/8" thick. The cover of a wallpaper catalog will work. (Peel off outside paper.) You could also use 1/8" plywood or a scrap of mat board which is used in picture framing.

Key Fob

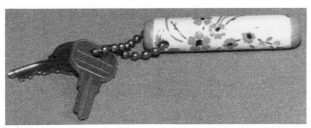

Illustration 56

DIRECTIONS FOR KEY FOB

1. Cut 3-3/4" off from a 1/4" dowel.
2. Round off ends and sand smooth.
3. Drill a 5/32" hole, 3/8" from end of dowel.
4. Paint dowel and dry overnight.
5. Glue on wallpaper.
6. After it's dry, clean out hole with a nail and attach key chain.

Candle Holder

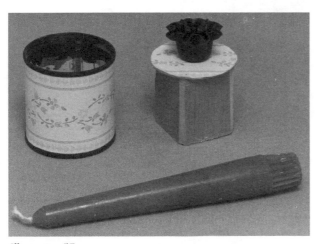

Illustration 57

MATERIALS FOR CANDLE HOLDER

2 oz. mushroom can, paint, piece of 2 by 2 (1-5/8" long), vinyl floor covering, scissors, glue, candle, damp cloth, utility knife, black candle holder and wallpaper.

DIRECTIONS FOR CANDLE HOLDER

1. Paint can black.
2. Glue a 2" circle of wallpaper and floor covering together. Dry overnight under weight.
3. Cut a piece of wallpaper 7" by 2" and glue on outside of can.
4. Round edges of wood to fit can.
5. Punch hole in center of circle, then put wood in vise and pilot a hole in center of wood.
6. Screw in candle holder and push into can.

Illustration 58

Jaguar Flowerpot

Illustration 59

A jaguar flowerpot is great for a den or office.
Just measure your pot and glue on wallpaper.

Jungle Artistry

Illustration 60

Cut a piece each of wallpaper and backing the size of
your frame. Glue or tape wallpaper to backing. Frame.
You can also use alligator, zebra or leopard designs.

Thread Rack

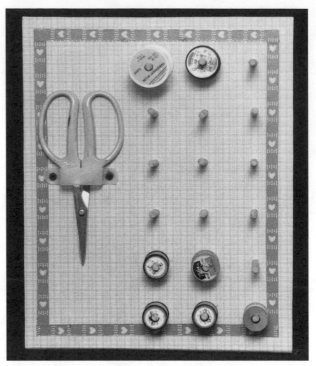

Illustration 61

MATERIALS FOR THREAD RACK

Ruler, wallpaper, 1/4" dowel, 3/8" thick plywood
or Masonite, scissors, glue, wallpaper trim and
damp cloth.

DIRECTIONS FOR THREAD RACK

1. Cut a piece of 3/8" thick Masonite 9-1/2" x 12".
2. Cut a piece of wallpaper 10" by 13". (This allows
   for overlap.)
3. Center wallpaper on board, snip corners and
   overlap to back.
4. Cut a piece of wallpaper 8-3/4" by 11-3/4" and glue
   on back of board.
5. Mark where you want the pegs.
6. Drill holes with a 1/4" drill.
7. Saw off 2" pegs from a 1/4" dowel. Put a dab of glue
   on end of each peg and push in holes.
8. Cut a plastic hanger for scissors. (See illustration
   61.) Secure hanger with small screws.
9. Glue a 1/2" border around sides.
10. Drill a hole through board and hang rack on a nail.

Bottle Vase

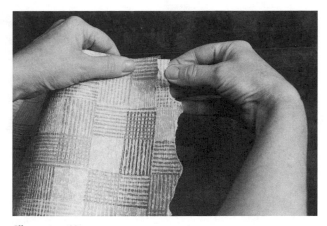

Illustration 62

Always tear strips of wallpaper toward you so that you don't get a white edge. Tear white edge off on the other side.

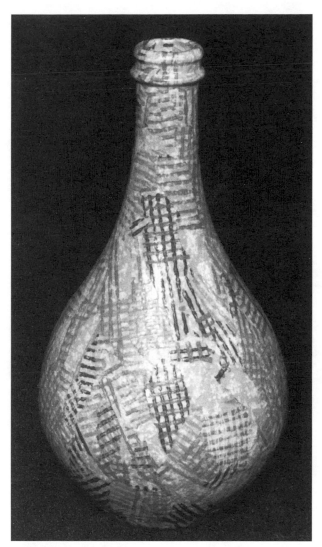

Illustration 64

MATERIALS FOR BOTTLE VASE
Bottle, damp cloth, brush, soft wallpaper with compact design and glue.

DIRECTIONS FOR BOTTLE VASE
1. Begin at the top of bottle, overlapping inside.
2. Use a damp cloth to keep hands and bottle free from glue.
3. Tear wider strips for the middle part of the vase. When you get to the bottom, tear thin strips to avoid wrinkles.
4. Dry overnight.
5. Glaze with thinned glue for a porcelain look.

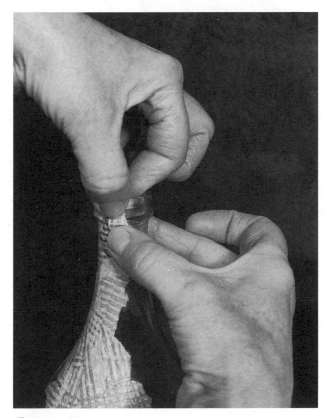

Illustration 63

Note the thin strips on the bottle neck. After the wallpaper has absorbed the glue, go back and press down again with the damp cloth.

Plant Vase/Notion Dish/Wide Mouth Vase

Illustration 65

Decor Vases

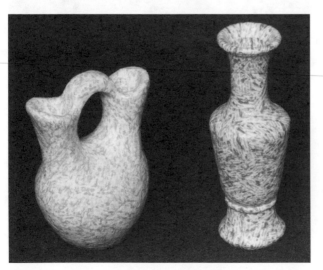

Illustration 66

PLANT VASE

Fill with water and slip in a vine to root. Check water level occasionally. This decanter was bought at a garage sale for 10¢.

NOTION DISH

Don't throw away your ash trays. Recycle them into an interesting notion dish.

WIDE MOUTH VASE

Fill this vase with an assortment of silk flowers. Choose colors that complement your vase.

These bright vases will brighten up any dull corner.
(See illustration 62 and 63 on page 29.)

Illustration 67

Pussy Willows/Gold-Trimmed Vase

MATERIALS FOR PUSSY WILLOWS

Small size chenille bumps, lilac stems with buds and brown floral tape.

DIRECTIONS FOR PUSSY WILLOWS

1. Cut chenille bumps so that you have a stem to wind tape on. (See illustration 67.)
2. Begin at top of stem, wind tape tightly around chenille bumps all the way down stem to 2" below top of vase.

MATERIALS FOR GOLD-TRIMMED VASE

Wallpaper with a compact design, small brush, damp cloth, scissors, fine sandpaper, gold paint, glue, utility knife and large glue jar.

DIRECTIONS FOR GOLD-TRIMMED VASE

1. Use a utility knife to cut off the top of a large glue jar.
2. Even off edge with a scissors. Smooth with sand-paper.
3. Begin at the top of jar. Tear a narrow strip of wallpaper, glue on jar, extending 1" inside. (See illustration 62 and 63 on page 29.)
4. Dry overnight.
5. Paint top edge of vase. Dry.
6. Glaze vase with thinned glue.

Illustration 68

Clothes Hamper

Illustration 69

This crazy quilt hamper can match a crazy quilt bedspread perfectly if you follow this simple rule: Outline hamper with the same color as the outline in your spread, and focus on the same color scheme as the bedspread.

NOTE

When outlining a crazy quilt project, choose a tame shade that blends with your wallpaper. I recommend any scale model paint because it cleans up with water, is odorless, and is permanent after it dries. Use 5/0 or 4/0 size brush.

MATERIALS FOR CLOTHES HAMPER

Garbage bag (11 gallon size), masking tape, brush for gluing, glue, damp cloth, assorted wallpaper, outline paint, enamel paint, size 5/0 brush for outlining, thumb tacks, scissors, barrel and knob for cover.

DIRECTIONS FOR CLOTHES HAMPER

1. Paint barrel hoops and knob.
2. Tape all cracks in barrel with masking tape.
3. Glue wallpaper on in a crazy quilt fashion. Remember to do the inside of top edge.
4. Outline pieces with scale model paint. Dry overnight.
5. Drill pilot hole in cover and attach knob.
6. Insert garbage bag, folding top down and fastening with tacks.
7. Glaze hamper with thinned glue.

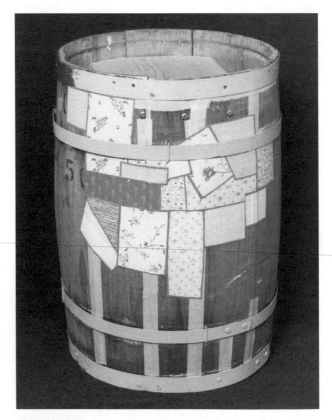

Illustration 70

NOTE

Reinforcement board at top of barrel adds support to the bedroom stool.

Bedroom Stool

Illustration 71

MATERIALS FOR BEDROOM STOOL

Glue, size 5/0 brush for outlining, enamel paint, assorted wallpaper, masking tape, scale model paint, six 1-1/4" long screws, and a 3/4" thick board to reinforce cover, measuring 7-1/2" wide by 12" long.

DIRECTIONS FOR BEDROOM STOOL

1. Use a coping saw to round off ends of reinforcement board to fit barrel.
2. Mark spots where screws line up with board and pilot holes on one side for screws. Twist in screws.
3. Then, do other side and tap in cover until it rests on board.
4. Paint barrel hoops with enamel paint and dry thoroughly.
5. Cover all cracks and edges with masking tape.
6. Glue wallpaper onto barrel in a crazy quilt fashion. Dry overnight.
7. Outline wallpaper pieces with scale model paint.
8. Let dry overnight, then glaze barrel with a coat of thinned glue.

MATERIALS FOR CUSHION

Needle and thread, 1/2 yd. of soft material, 1' square of foam cushion (1" thick), ruler and scissors.

DIRECTIONS FOR CUSHION

1. Cut a 12" circle from the foam cushion square.
2. Next, cut two 13-1/2" circles from your material.
3. Place the circles together with right sides facing each other. Sew a 3/8" hem around edge, leaving a 5" opening to insert cushion.
4. Then, turn material right side out and press seam.
5. Insert cushion and sew opening closed with small stitches and the same color thread as the material.

NOTE

The diameter of barrel is 12" and is 18-1/2" high.

Handkerchief Box

Brick Bookends

Illustration 72

MATERIALS FOR HANDKERCHIEF BOX

5/0 size brush for outlining, scissors, cigar box, brush for gluing, scale model paint, damp cloth, light and dark wallpaper, small knob for lid and glue.

DIRECTIONS FOR HANDKERCHIEF BOX

1. Remove loose paper from cigar box.
2. Glue wallpaper around edges before doing the center.
3. Then, continue over rest of box in a crazy quilt fashion.
4. When finished, dry overnight.
5. Outline pieces with scale model paint. Use color that matches the wallpaper.
6. If screw for knob is too long, saw it off to fit width of cover.
7. Drill small pilot hole in the center of cover, 1/2" from edge.
8. Insert knob.

The handkerchief box was made with tan and dark brown wallpaper. Medium brown paint was used for outlining.

Illustration 73

DIRECTIONS FOR BOOKENDS

1. Fill in any chips with spackling. Let dry.
2. Glue assorted wallpaper to the edge first, then complete with rest in a crazy quilt fashion.
3. Dry overnight.
4. Outline pieces with scale model paint. Glaze when thoroughly dry.

Illustration 74

Crazy Quilt Wastebasket

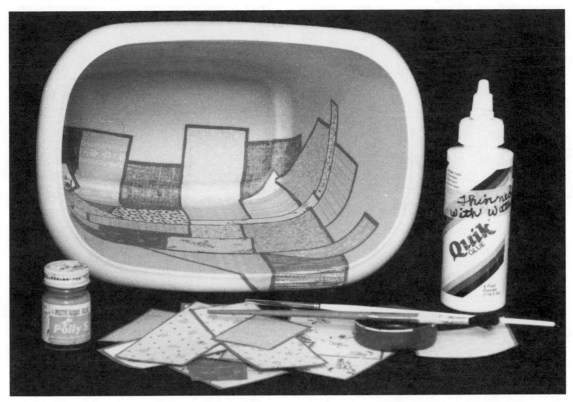

Illustration 75

MATERIALS FOR CRAZY QUILT WASTEBASKET

Scale model paint, assorted wallpaper, glue, scissors, size 5/0 brush for outlining, wastebasket, larger brush for gluing and cover for glue.

DIRECTIONS FOR CRAZY QUILT WASTEBASKET

1. Cut assorted sizes and shapes of wallpaper.
2. Outline pieces with scale model paint. Dry overnight.
3. Now, glue pieces onto wastebasket in crazy quilt fashion, overlapping edges. Dry overnight.
4. Glaze with thinned glue.

NOTE

Outline the inside pieces before you glue them on, because it is impossible to outline inside of wastebasket.

Illustration 76

Line wastebasket with small plastic bag to keep inside clean.

Memento Box

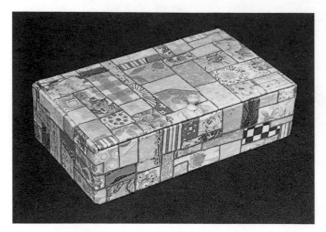

Illustration 77

MATERIALS FOR MEMENTO BOX

Assorted wallpaper, scale model paint, 5/0 size brush for outlining, scissors, gluing brush, small knob for cover and damp cloth.

DIRECTIONS FOR MEMENTO BOX

1. Glue wallpaper around all edges first, then complete rest of box. Dry overnight.
2. Outline pieces with scale model paint, using a medium blue. Dry overnight
3. Pilot a hole in center of cover 1/2" from edge. Insert knob. Saw off screw to fit thickness of cover.
4. Glaze box with thinned glue.

Illustration 78

This roomy box will hold all your trinkets and souvenirs.

Key Dish

Illustration 79

MATERIALS FOR KEY DISH

Large cover, assorted wallpaper, brush for gluing, pinking shears for cutting wallpaper, glue and damp cloth.

DIRECTIONS FOR KEY DISH

1. Cut assorted, pliable wallpaper (not vinyl) with pinking shears and glue on cover in a crazy quilt fashion.
2. Dry overnight, then glaze with thinned glue.

NOTE

An Eucerine jar cover is just the right size and rust proof.

Crazy Quilt Necklace Tree

Crazy Quilt Vase

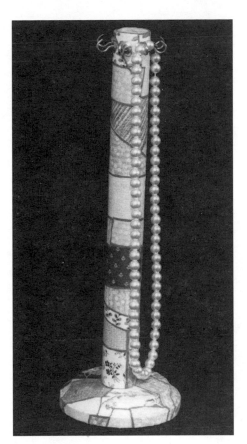

Illustration 80

Illustration 81

MATERIALS FOR CRAZY QUILT NECKLACE TREE

Glue, 1" dowel, 3-1/2" plaque, 8 cup hooks, 1-1/2" wood screw, assorted wallpaper, 5/0 size brush for outlining, scale model paint, damp cloth, scissors and gluing brush.

DIRECTIONS FOR CRAZY QUILT NECKLACE TREE

1. Cut a 10-1/2" piece off a 1" dowel and glue wallpaper on it, in crazy quilt fashion.
2. Do same for the top of plaque.
3. Pilot hole for screw and attach plaque to dowel.
4. Outline wallpaper pieces with scale model paint. Dry overnight.
5. Glaze with thinned glue. Dry.
6. Pilot holes with small nail, 1/2" from top and 1/4" apart. Twist cup screws in.
7. Glue felt on bottom of plaque.

MATERIALS FOR CRAZY QUILT VASE

Flowers, brush for gluing, 5/0 size brush for outlining, scale model paint, assorted wallpaper, bottle, damp cloth, scissors and glue.

DIRECTIONS FOR CRAZY QUILT VASE

1. Glue pieces of wallpaper onto bottle in crazy quilt fashion.
2. Dry overnight.
3. Outline pieces with paint and dry overnight.
4. Then, glaze with thinned glue.

Magazine Rack

Illustration 82

Illustration 83

The container in illustration 82 measures 12" in diameter and 15" high. The divider must be the same width as the inside of can to assure a tight fit.

Hardware stores and factories often receive bulk products in large cans like the one in illustration 82. Most of them can be recycled into attractive magazine racks and wastebaskets.

DIRECTIONS FOR INSTALLING HANDLE

1. Place handle on top center of divider and mark screw holes.
2. Pilot holes and attach handle with screws.

MATERIALS FOR MAGAZINE RACK

Large can, vinyl wallcovering paste, 1/2" thick piece of plywood, yardstick, vinyl wallpaper, brush, paint and handle.

DIRECTIONS FOR MAGAZINE RACK

1. Paint handle, rims and bottom of can. Dry overnight.
2. Then, measure height inside of can. Paste wallpaper on inside of can in three pieces. (It's next to impossible to get it pasted on in one piece without wrinkles.)
3. Do the same on the outside. Be sure to match pattern at seams.
4. Cut a piece of plywood 12" by 12".
5. Paste a piece of wallpaper over top of divider. (See illustration 83.)
6. Now, cut out two more pieces of wallpaper, one for each side. Do not overlap paper.

DIRECTIONS FOR INSTALLING DIVIDER

1. Bend top of can slightly, using your knees and slide divider down center of can.
2. After pressure is released, the divider is firmly fixed.

Umbrella Stand

Illustration 84

MATERIALS FOR UMBRELLA STAND

1-1/2" brush, vinyl wallpaper, yardstick, two 3-lb. coffee cans, duct tape, small pebbles to stabilize stand, glue, and scissors.

DIRECTIONS FOR UMBRELLA STAND

1. Cut out the bottom of a coffee can and spray paint top rim. Spray paint bottom and rim of other can.
2. Cut a piece of wallpaper 6-1/2" by 20" and glue inside of bottom can.
3. Cut a piece of duct tape 20" long, and tape bottomless can on top of other can. Then, tape them together on the inside.
4. Cut a piece of wallpaper 7-1/2" by 20". Glue to top inside of stand. This allows enough to cover tape.
5. Cut another piece of wallpaper 13-1/2" by 20" and glue on outside of coffee cans.
6. Trim the stand with horizontal strips of wallpaper.
7. Stabilize stand by lining bottom with two inches of pebbles.
8. Cover pebbles with a 5-3/4" circle of mat board. (optional)

Extension Cord Holder

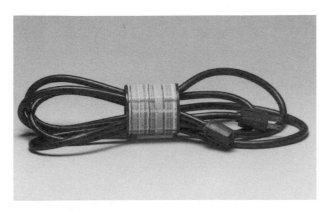

Illustration 85

MATERIALS FOR CORD HOLDER

A small can about 2" in diameter, wallpaper, scissors, ruler, spray paint, damp cloth and glue.

DIRECTIONS FOR CORD HOLDER

1. Cut bottom from can, Remove all paper, wash and dry can.
2. Hang on clothesline outdoors to spray paint can inside and outside. Dry well.
3. Glue vinyl wallpaper on outside of can.
4. Install square-bend screw hooks in wall and hang by cord loops.

Napkin Holder

Illustration 86

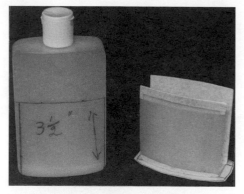

Illustration 87

The napkin holder is made from a plastic Cetaphil bottle. There are other flat bottles that will work but be sure the plastic is soft enough to cut safely and smoothly.

MATERIALS FOR NAPKIN HOLDER

Glue, Cetaphil bottle (liquid soap), ruler, vinyl wallpaper, marker, damp cloth and scissors.

DIRECTIONS FOR NAPKIN HOLDER

1. Rinse out bottle with warm water, and tip upside down to drain.
2. Use a black marker to mark off 3-1/2" on both sides of bottle. (See illustration 87.)
3. Cut off top of bottle, then cut out sides to create a napkin holder.
4. Cut two pieces of wallpaper, 1" by 4-1/2" and glue over top of each side. Snip corners and fold over.
5. Then, trace two bottoms of napkin holder, allowing 1/2" overlap on all sides. (See illustration 87.)
6. Glue one inside of bottom, snip corners and overlap ends.
7. Do same for outside bottom.
8. Cut two pieces of wallpaper 3-3/8" by 8-3/4". Glue onto sides of napkin holder, with the seams inside.
9. Dry overnight.

Photo Paperweight

Illustration 88

MATERIALS FOR PHOTO PAPERWEIGHT

A 12 oz. coffee jar cover, photo, plaster of Paris, glue, wallpaper, vinyl floor covering, paint, scissors and 5/0 brush for outlining.

DIRECTIONS FOR PHOTO PAPERWEIGHT

1. Mix plaster according to directions. Fill cover 3/4 full.
2. Make a plastic pattern of a 2-7/8" circle. Center pattern over photo. Trace and cut out photo.
3. Using pattern, cut one each of floor covering and wallpaper. Glue the wallpaper on the wrong side of floor covering. Dry under weight.
4. Trace a 3/8" border around wallpaper and cut out center. This is a frame for your photo. Paint edge of frame. Dry well.

Floral Centerpiece

Illustration 90

MATERIALS FOR FLORAL CENTERPIECE

Plaster of Paris, white spray can cover, small silk flowers, wallpaper, scissors, glue and moss.

DIRECTIONS FOR FLORAL CENTERPIECE

1. Cut flower stems to 4".
2. Mix plaster according to directions and fill cover 3/4 full.
3. Insert flower stems when plaster begins to thicken.
4. Glue wallpaper around cover.
5. Cover plaster with floral moss.

Napkin Holder

Illustration 89

MATERIALS FOR NAPKIN HOLDER

Glue, a repair tape core 1-1/2" in diameter and 2" wide, ruler, wallpaper, scissors and damp cloth.

DIRECTIONS FOR NAPKIN HOLDER

1. Glue a piece of wallpaper 2" by 6" around a 2" wide tape core.
2. Make five more for a set of six.

Heart Napkin Holder

Illustration 91

DIRECTIONS FOR HEART NAPKIN HOLDER

1. Paint core black to match vase on page 15. Glue on white wallpaper.
2. Add hearts cut from wallpaper.

Magnetic Butterfly

Illustration 92

MATERIALS FOR MAGNETIC BUTTERFLY

Magnetic tape, thinned glue, wallpaper, stamens for butterfly antennae, toothpick and brush.

DIRECTIONS FOR MAGNETIC BUTTERFLY

1. Glue two pieces of wallpaper back to back using thinned glue. Dry under board overnight.
2. Trace butterfly onto wallpaper and cut out.
3. Now trace two black bodies for each butterfly and cut them out. (See patterns on page 43.)
4. Glue a body on front side of butterfly.
5. Turn butterfly over. Cut a stamen in two and glue on the head of butterfly for antennae.
6. Next, glue other body over the antennae. Gently, press the two bodies together without moving antennae out of place. Let dry.
7. Cut a small piece of magnetic tape. Use unthinned glue, and glue magnet to back of butterfly. Leave flat until dry.
8. Cut between wings, just to the edge of body and gently bend top wings up. (See patterns, page 43.)

NOTE

A toothpick can be used as a guide to glue on antennae. Use the glue without thinning to glue on magnet because it dries quicker. You will find the Small Butterfly pattern on page 13.

Illustration 93

Patterns for Magnetic Butterfly

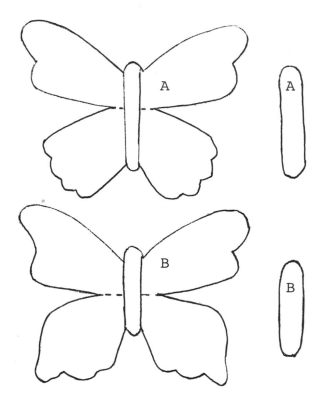

Wallpaper Doily

Illustration 95

Directions for Wallpaper Doily

1. Choose wallpaper with a raised pattern that looks like cloth.
2. Use a paper doily as a pattern and trace onto wallpaper
3. Cut out doily.

Toothpick Holder

Illustration 94

Directions for Toothpick Holder

1. Wash a 35 mm film canister and dry.
2. Use wallpaper with a miniature pattern in a color scheme matching your table setting.
3. Cut a strip of wallpaper 5" by 1-3/4" and glue on canister. Leave a black edge on bottom to match top. It makes a balanced composition.

Tieback Pin

Illustration 96

Illustration 97

MATERIALS FOR TIEBACK PIN
Wallpaper flower image, Congoleum, glue, upholstery tacks, damp cloth, gluing brush and scissors.

DIRECTIONS FOR TIEBACK PIN
1. Choose front view of a flower so you can put a tack in the center.
2. Place flower on wrong side of Congoleum and trace around it.
3. Cut out and glue together.
4. Dry overnight under weight.
5. Press upholstery tack through center of flower.
6. Outline flower with a permanent marker to set off the petals and create a more striking design.

NOTE
Make the tieback pin out of leftover wallpaper from your wall so it will match (See the upholstery tack in center of flowers.)

Coasters

MATERIALS FOR COASTERS
Wallpaper, plastic cover from a baking powder or potato chip can, glue, Congoleum, damp cloth, brush and scissors.

DIRECTIONS FOR COASTERS
1. Any item that is 3" or 4" around can be used for pattern. A water glass or custard cup is fine.
2. Cut out one each of vinyl wallpaper and Congoleum.
3. Glue wallpaper circle onto the wrong side of Congoleum circle.
4. Dry under weight overnight.
5. Optional: A 3" coaster will fit into a potato chip canister cover.

Illustration 98

Oval Place Mat

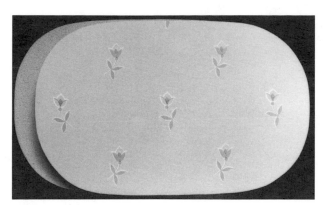

Illustration 99

Octagon Place Mat

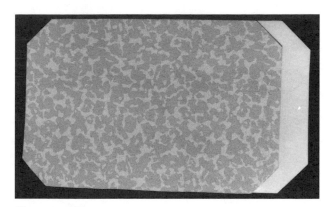

Illustration 100

MATERIALS FOR PLACE MATS

Wallpaper, scissors, vinyl floor covering, damp cloth and glue.

DIRECTIONS FOR PLACE MATS

1. Use an old place mat and trace shape onto vinyl floor covering, and another using vinyl wallcovering.
2. Next, glue the wallpaper on the wrong side of the floor covering.
3. Use damp cloth to press out air bubbles. Place two paper towels over place mat and dry under weight overnight.

NOTE

It would be especially nice if your mats matched the wallpaper on your walls. Make as many place mats as you have place settings.

Doorstop

MATERIALS FOR DOORSTOP

Lined vinyl wallpaper, damp cloth, ruler, Spackle, brick, scissors and glue.

DIRECTIONS FOR DOORSTOP

1. Apply Spackle to any small chip on brick.
2. Cut a piece of wallpaper 9-1/2" by 13-1/2". (This allows for overlap.)
3. Apply glue to wallpaper. Stand brick in center and bring wallpaper up to top. Now bring the other side up and overlap. (See illustration 101.)
4. Snip end corners. Then, overlap ends. Press down all sides.
5. Cut a strip of wallpaper 1-1/4" by 15". Glue around center of brick. (This will cover top seam and bare spots on ends.)

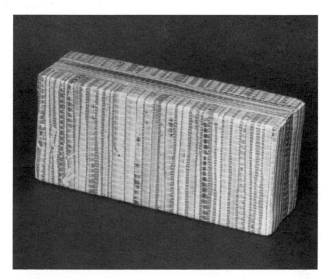

Illustration 101

Bulletin Board

Illustration 102

Illustration 103

MATERIALS FOR BULLETIN BOARD

Push pins, corrugated cardboard, scissors, thinned glue, masking tape, old leather purse for reinforcement rings, paper punch, string, brush, wallpaper and yardstick.

DIRECTIONS FOR BULLETIN BOARD

1. Cut four pieces of corrugated cardboard 14" by 16".
2. Glue them together with thinned glue. Dry overnight, then tape edges.
3. Cut a plain piece of wallpaper 18" by 20". Apply glue to it.
4. Center cardboard on wallpaper. Fold over sides, snip corners and fold over ends. (Illustration 102)
5. Cut a piece of wallpaper 13-7/8" by 15-7/8" and glue on back. Let dry overnight.
6. Punch holes for string.
7. Make leather reinforcements for holes and glue on front and back.
8. Thread string through holes and glue wallpaper flowers in corners.

Big and Little Dipper

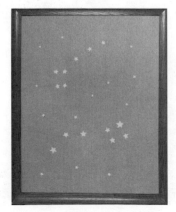

Illustration 104

DIRECTIONS FOR BIG AND LITTLE DIPPER PICTURE

1. Cut a piece each of blue wallpaper and corrugated cardboard the size of your frame.
2. Glue wallpaper onto cardboard.
3. Cut stars from yellow paper.
4. Carefully arrange stars on blue wallpaper. (Copy pattern from an astronomy book in library.) Apply glue to stars and press down with damp cloth.
5. Frame when dry.

Genealogy Can

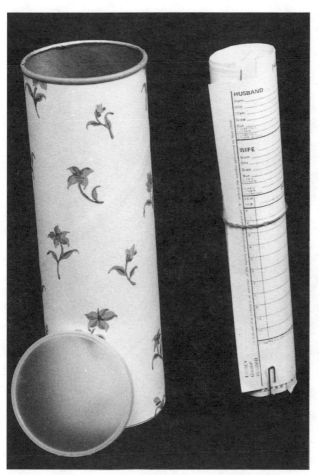

Illustration 105

Materials for Genealogy Can

Glue, thinned glue, scissors, wallpaper, potato chip can, ruler and damp cloth.

Directions for Genealogy Can

1. Cans vary in size, so measure height and circumference of your can.
2. Cut wallpaper according to the size of your can and glue onto can.
3. Wipe surface glue off and press out air bubbles with a damp cloth.
4. Roll up your genealogy records in a small roll, put a rubber band around them and put into can. (See illustration 105.)

Note

Store small doilies in can by winding them around the cardboard core of a plastic wrap. Cut off core to fit can. (Secure each doily with a stickpin.)

Wallpaper Bands

Directions for Wallpaper Bands

1. Cut strips of vinyl wallpaper 1-1/2" wide and as long as needed.
2. Glue, staple or pin the bands together.
3. Use a permanent marker to write size and type on band.
4. After row covers are folded and banded, stack in cardboard box or brown bag.

Note

Row covers are used to protect plants from frost and insects. Row covers will last for years if taken care of. When season is over, wash on gentle cycle and hang on line. Fold and band.

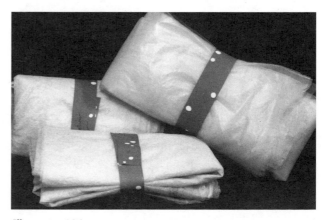

Illustration 106

Tote Bag

Illustration 107

MATERIALS FOR TOTE BAG

Brown bag with a bottom size 5" by 8", vinyl wallpaper, yardstick, brush, glue, scissors and damp cloth.

DIRECTIONS FOR TOTE BAG

1. Cut bag to 10" high.
2. Cut a strip of wallpaper 1-1/2" by 30".
3. Fold over and crease center of wallpaper, lengthwise, then flatten out again and apply glue.
4. Place strip over top of bag and push down to the crease. Press down sides of trim with a damp cloth.
5. Now cut a strip for the handle 1-3/4" by 16".
6. Crease and fold over both sides 1/2". (They overlap in middle.)
7. Next, apply glue and fold over both sides on crease again.
8. Apply glue to 2" of each end of handle and glue on inside of bag.
9. Put paper clips over a handle until glue dries.
10. Cut two patches of brown paper 2" by 3-1/2". Glue over ends of handle, even with trim.
11. Glue matching flowers on bag. (See illustration 107.)

MATERIALS FOR PROTECTIVE BOTTOM

Thin cardboard, a piece of window plastic, scissors and stapler.

DIRECTIONS FOR PROTECTIVE BOTTOM

1. Trace pattern and cut out.
2. Cut on black lines, score and fold on dotted lines.
3. Then, cut facsimile out of plastic and cut on black lines.
4. Put plastic inside of box, fold with cardboard and staple in the corners.

NOTE

The plastic bottom protects the bag when carrying damp items like ice cream or plants.

Pattern for Tote Bag's Protective Bottom

Cut on black line. Score on dotted line, then fold toward you.

(Trace facsimile out of heavy plastic and cut on black line.)

Telephone Accessory

Illustration 108

MATERIALS FOR TELEPHONE ACCESSORY

1/2 gallon milk carton, masking tape, piece of 2 by 4, a piece of cardboard 1/8" thick, vinyl wallpaper, 5/16" spade bit, utility knife, note pad, scissors, damp cloth and ruler.

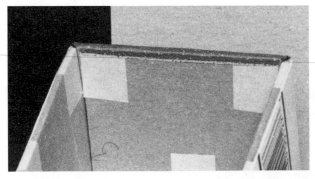

Illustration 109

Cut the ends of strip at an angle so the sides butt together in the corners like a picture frame. (See illustration 109.)

DIRECTIONS ON TELEPHONE ACCESSORY

1. Cut off milk carton to 3" high.
2. Cut two pieces of cardboard 1/8" thick, 3" by 3-3/8".
3. Cut two more pieces 3" by 3-3/4".
4. Slide the two widest pieces in box first on opposite sides. Tape across top and bottom to hold in.
5. Tape in the short pieces on the remaining sides.
6. Now, cut four strips of wallpaper for top edge of box, 3-3/4" long and 5/8" wide.
7. Glue a strip over the top of each side. Cut ends at an angle so they butt together in the corners like a picture frame.
8. Cut a piece of wallpaper 15-1/2" by 4-1/8" for outside of box.
9. Glue on outside of box, cut corners and overlap on bottom. (See illustration 111.)
10. Next, cut a piece of wallpaper for inside of box 3" by 13-1/2". Cut piece in half and glue on in two pieces.
11. Cut two pieces for the outside and inside bottom of box 3-3/8" by 3-3/8" and glue on.

Illustration 110

NOTE

You can line milk carton with mat board, 1/8" thick cardboard or plywood.

Telephone Mat

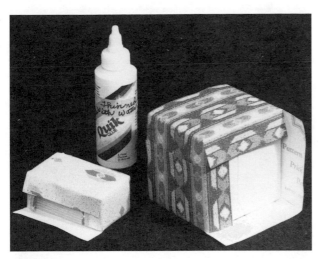

Illustration 111

DIRECTIONS FOR PENCIL HOLDER

1. Saw a piece of wood from a 2 by 4, 3-3/8" long and 2-1/8" high.
2. Bevel top edges 1/4".
3. Sand smooth.
4. Drill three pencil holes 1-1/2" deep, across center of wood with a 5/16" spade bit.
5. Cut a piece of wallpaper 2-1/2" wide by 4-1/8" long for holder top. Glue over holes, snip corners and overlap.
6. Cut another piece, 10-1/4" by 2-1/2" and glue around sides of pencil holder. Cut corners and overlap on bottom.
7. When holder is dry, use a utility knife to cut out pencil holes.
8. Glue a 1/2" wide trim around the top of box. (see illustration 111.)
9. Now arrange the items in box. First, put in pencil holder, then address book and note pad behind.

NOTE

Coordinate the color of your wallpaper to the surrounding color scheme of your room.

Illustration 112

MATERIALS FOR TELEPHONE MAT

Glue, a piece of Masonite 7" by 11" and 3/16" thick, vinyl wallpaper, ruler, scissors and brush.

DIRECTIONS FOR TELEPHONE MAT

1. Cut a piece of wallpaper 12" by 8" and glue onto board. Snip corners and overlap to back.
2. Cut a piece of wallpaper 10-7/8" by 6-7/8" and glue on back.

NOTE

Your particular telephone may not fit the mat. Adjust size of Masonite and wallpaper accordingly.

Jewelry Box

Illustration 113

Illustration 114

MATERIALS FOR JEWELRY BOX

Covered cigar box, scissors, poster board, thinned glue and felt.

DIRECTIONS FOR JEWELRY BOX

1. Follow directions at right for covering cigar box.
2. Cut a piece of cardboard 8-3/8" by 9-7/8".
3. Follow dimensions from illustration 115 and pencil in lines.
4. Score lines with dull knife and bend. *Dotted* lines must be scored on reverse side and bent.
5. Now, cut a strip 3" by 16-1/4".
6. Use dimensions from illustration 115 and draw lines, Score and bend cardboard.
7. Next, lay both cardboards flat and apply thinned glue.
8. Place felt over glue and press down. Dry overnight.
9. Bend dividers where scored. Put lengthwise divider in first, then the narrow one in back side.

NOTE

The box used in illustration 114 was 2-1/2" high, 8-3/4" long, and 6" wide. If your box is different, adjust dividers to fit.

MATERIALS FOR COVERING CIGAR BOX

Small knob, vinyl wallpaper, glue, cigar box, brush, ruler and scissors.

DIRECTIONS FOR COVERING CIGAR BOX

1. Measure a piece of vinyl wallpaper long enough to go around cigar box and overlap 1-1/2" on sides and bottom. (See illustration 114.)
2. Cut inside, side pieces. Allow 1" overlap on sides and bottom.
3. Cut and glue on final piece for inside, beginning at top of cover, going all the way to inside top of front. (If you prefer, glue it on in two pieces.)
4. Pilot a hole in center of cover 1/2" from edge. Then, drill hole. If screw is too long, saw it off.
5. Insert knob.

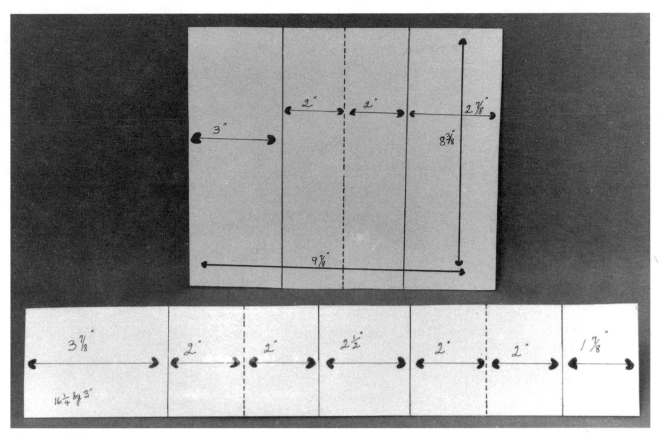

Illustration 115

Score all solid lines on the front side, but the three dotted lines must be scored and bent on the reverse side.

Illustration 116

Before you glue on the felt put dividers into cigar box to see how they fit. When felt is dry put a little glue between cardboard under the paper clips.

Money Box

Coin Jar

Illustration 117

Illustration 118

MATERIALS FOR MONEY BOX

Scissors, an 8 oz. shampoo bottle, wallpaper, cardboard box, utility knife, masking tape and glue.

DIRECTIONS FOR MONEY BOX

1. Cut the cover threads off an 8 oz. plastic shampoo bottle.

2. Next cut in half, lengthwise.

3. Tape on cardboard ends to cover up cap hole and to achieve a snug fit for coin receptacle.

4. Trace around end to get pattern for cardboard pieces. Put one on inside of each end and as many as needed on the outside for a tight fit in box. Tape pieces together with masking tape. (See illustration 117.)

5. Cover outside ends with wallpaper, overlapping edges. Next cut two pieces the size of cardboard and glue on the inside of ends.

6. Then, cut a piece for outside of coin receptacle, long enough so it overlaps on the inside top on both sides.

7. Measure a shorter piece for the inside and glue on.

NOTE

Box in illustration 119 is 5" by 6-1/2". Directions for covering cigar box are on page 52.

The coin jar is made from a 16 oz. Eucerin hand cream jar. Cut a piece of wallpaper 12" by 2-1/4" and glue on outside of jar.

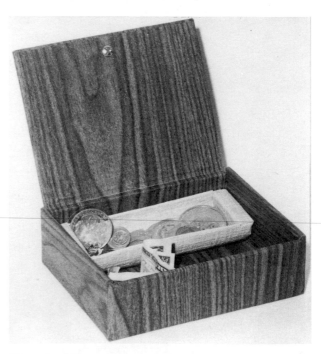

Illustration 119

Notion Jar

Illustration 120

DIRECTIONS FOR NOTION JARS

1. Paint cover to match wallpaper.
2. Measure height and circumference of jar. Cut out wallpaper and glue on jar.

Embroidery Floss Canister

Illustration 121

The 6" high jar shown in illustration 121 is roomy enough to hold all your embroidery floss. It came from a dental office and all this jar needed to brighten it up was a few wallpaper decals.

Knee-High Cannikin

Illustration 122

MATERIALS FOR KNEE-HIGH CANNIKIN

Plastic or tin container, wallpaper, small knob, scissors, paint for knob, ruler, glue and damp cloth.

DIRECTIONS FOR KNEE-HIGH CANNIKIN

1. Paint knob to match wallpaper.
2. Drill hole through cover before you glue on the wallpaper.
3. Make a pattern for the wallpaper on cover. Cut out and glue onto cover. Then, cut a piece of wallpaper for outside of can.
4. Glue outside piece on and dry overnight.
5. Poke a small nail through drill hole from inside of cover.
6. Screw on knob.

NOTE

The container in illustration 122 will hold several pair of knee-high nylons. It opens easily with a knob.

Silk Wallpaper Bank

Illustration 123

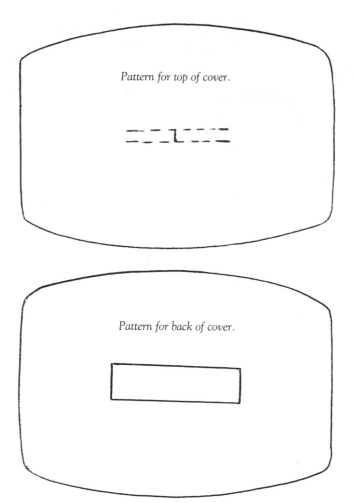

Pattern for top of cover.

Pattern for back of cover.

MATERIALS FOR SILK WALLPAPER BANK

X-acto knife, small cocoa can, ruler, silk wallpaper, brush, scissors and damp cloth.

DIRECTIONS FOR SILK WALLPAPER BANK

1. Cut a 1" slit in center of cover. Use scissors to widen to 1/8".
2. Use pattern to cut out wallpaper for the top. (Do not cut out hole yet.) Glue on top of cover.
3. Dry overnight.
4. Lay cover on board, backside up. Cut on dotted lines with X-acto knife. Push tabs through to back and glue down.

5. Now, make a facing for opening. Cut a strip of wallpaper 1" by 7/16". Fold in center lengthwise and glue on side. Do other side likewise.
6. Glue a small strip over ends.
7. Cut out wallpaper for backside of cover. Cut out hole, then glue wallpaper on back of cover.
8. Cut two pieces of wallpaper 3-7/8" by 12". Glue one on the inside and the other on the outside of can.

Illustration 124

Nature Bank

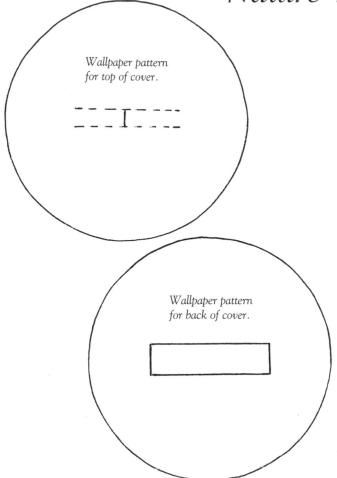

Wallpaper pattern for top of cover.

Wallpaper pattern for back of cover.

Illustration 125

MATERIALS FOR NATURE BANK

A large Calument baking powder can, X-acto knife, wild fowl images, glue, ruler, scissors, solid color wallpaper, brush and damp cloth.

DIRECTIONS FOR NATURE BANK

1. Use X-acto knife to cut slit in center of cover, 3-3/16" by 1-1/8".

2. Cut wallpaper for top of cover. (Do not cut out hole yet.) Glue on cover and dry overnight.

3. Place cover on board (backside up) then cut, where indicated by dotted lines with X-acto knife. Push tabs through to back and glue down.

4. Make a facing for opening. Cut two strips of wallpaper 1-1/8" long and 7/16" wide. Fold in half lengthwise and glue on side. Do the other side and glue strips over ends.

5. Cut out wallpaper for the backside of cover. Cut hole out, then glue piece on back of cover.

6. Cut two pieces of wallpaper 5" by 10". Glue on inside and outside of can.

7. Glue images on can.

Decorative Rock

Illustration 126

Glue a piece of magnetic tape onto an interesting rock. Refer to page 42 for directions on making a butterfly. (Glue felt on rock bottom.)

Cover Pincushion

Illustration 129

Illustration 127

Illustration 128

MATERIALS FOR PINCUSHION

Pliable wallpaper with miniature design, a piece of 1-1/2" thick foam rubber, cover, black velvet, small brush, utility knife, scissors, glue and a damp cloth.

DIRECTIONS FOR PINCUSHION

1. Cut a 6-1/2" circle from a piece of black velvet.
2. Baste 1/4" hem around the edge of circle. Thread string through hem.
3. Now cut a 2-3/4" circle from a 1-1/2" thick foam rubber, using a utility knife.
4. Round top slightly and trim the sides with a scissors.
5. Place foam rubber (rounded end down) inside of velvet. Pull ends of string tight and tie a bow.

DIRECTIONS FOR COVER BASE

1. Use pliable wallpaper that has a miniature design. (See illustration 127.)
2. Glue wallpaper on in strips. To learn the technique, turn to page 29.

NOTE

After the cover is finished let it dry overnight. Glaze inside and outside top half. Dry well and glaze bottom outside half. (Dry upside down.) It will shine like pottery when dry.

Sewing Set

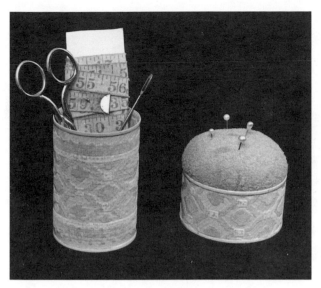

Illustration 130

MATERIALS FOR PINCUSHION

Utility knife, 2-1/2" thick foam rubber, soft material, wrapping string, ribbon threader, glue, needle and thread, scissors and 8 oz. pineapple can.

DIRECTIONS FOR PINCUSHION

1. Use a utility knife to cut a 3" circle from a 2-1/2" thick piece of foam rubber.
2. Round top slightly with a scissors and smooth sides.
3. Cut a 9" circle from soft material.
4. Sew a narrow hem around circle.
5. Thread string through hem.
6. Place foam rubber on inside of circle and draw string tight. Tie string in bow and place in base.

MATERIALS FOR SEWING CAN

Flocked wallpaper, damp cloth, ruler, soup can, glue, scissors and brush.

DIRECTIONS FOR SEWING CAN

1. Cut two pieces of flocked wallpaper 8-3/4" by 3-11/16".
2. Glue on the outside and inside of soup can.
3. Cut two 2-1/2" circles of wallpaper for inside and outside bottom of can. Press inside wallpaper down with eraser end of pencil.

DIRECTIONS FOR PINCUSHION BASE

1. Cut a piece of flocked wallpaper 1-9/16" by 11-1/2" and glue on outside of an 8 oz. pineapple can.
2. Cut a 3-1/4" circle and glue onto bottom of can.

NOTE

Disguise the tinny look by painting the cans. It will also keep them from rusting.

Heart Pincushion

Illustration 131

DIRECTIONS FOR HEART PINCUSHION

1. Follow above directions on making the pincushion.
2. Embroider white hearts around center of material before threading string through hem.
3. Place foam rubber on inside of circle and draw string tight. Tie string in bow and place in base.

Flowerpot Saucer

Dipper/Funnel

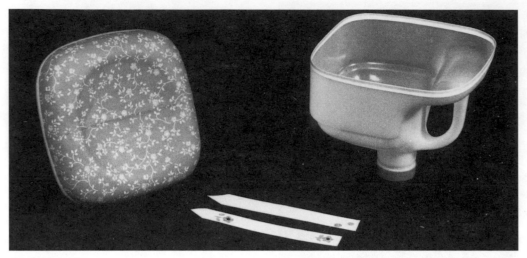

Illustration 132

DIRECTIONS FOR FLOWERPOT SAUCER

1. Use utility knife to cut off 7/8" of the bottom of a water jug.
2. Next, trace pattern on wallpaper and cut out.
3. Cut corners on dotted lines and cut wallpaper in half.
4. Glue half of wallpaper on. Use middle line in bottom of jug as a guide. Do other side and overlap.
5. Now cut a trim for top edge, 1" wide and 21" long. Crease in half lengthwise. (It's easier to glue on in two pieces.)
6. Lay flat and apply glue.
7. Fit crease on edge and press on both sides. Wipe with damp cloth.

DIRECTIONS FOR FUNNEL AND DIPPER

1. Cut the top off of a water jug, 3/4" below handle. Glue on trim.
2. Put cap on jug and use as a dipper or a quart measure for gardening nutrients. Make garden markers with the rest of the plastic.

Night Lamp Shade

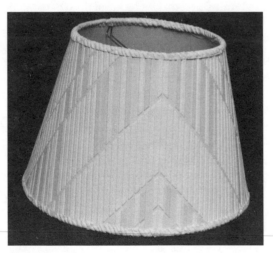

Illustration 133

DIRECTIONS FOR NIGHT LAMP SHADE

1. Make a pattern by rolling shade full circle across the paper while sketching the outline of shade.
2. Cut out your shade from wallpaper with same design as the walls.
3. Glue over old shade.
4. Cut a 5/8" strip of wallpaper for trim on bottom and top.

NOTE

The extra covering darkens the light somewhat, making a nice night light. Use a 15-watt bulb.

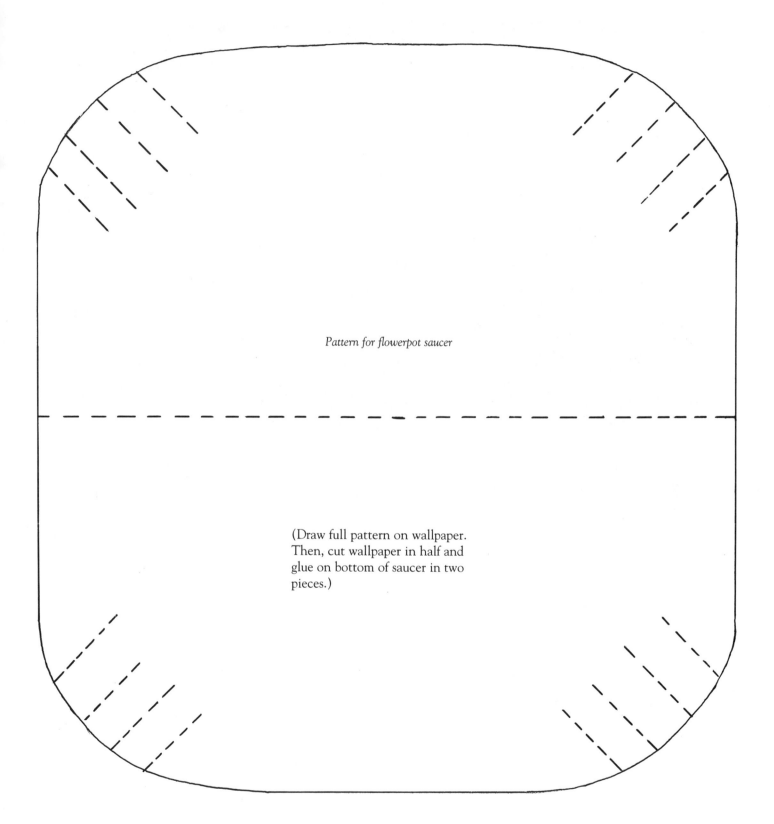

Pattern for flowerpot saucer

(Draw full pattern on wallpaper. Then, cut wallpaper in half and glue on bottom of saucer in two pieces.)

Paperback Bookcase

Illustration 134

MATERIALS FOR PAPERBACK BOOKCASE

A box 25" high, wallpaper, brush, yardstick, wallpaper paste, ruler, scissors, utility knife, masking tape and damp cloth.

DIRECTIONS FOR PAPERBACK BOOKCASE

1. Cut a piece of wallpaper, 26-1/2" long and 15-1/2" wide for back and outside bottom.
2. Apply wallpaper paste. Start at outside top back, overlapping 3/4" inside. Press wallpaper down well across back and bottom, overlapping 3/4" on sides and bottom. Snip corners and fold over sides.
3. Cut a piece for inside of bookcase, 25-3/4" long and 13-1/4" wide. Snip corners and overlap on sides.
4. Then, cut a piece for inside, side, allowing enough paper for 3/4" overlap to outside. Do other side.
5. Last, cut pieces for outside, sides and paste on. (No overlap is necessary here.)

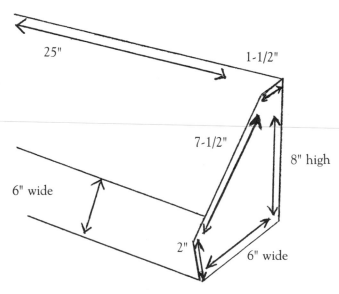

NOTE

Follow the diagram above and cut out your bookcase. If box is not 25" high, simply adjust length of wallpaper accordingly. To get a smooth edge, tape all edges with masking tape before you put on the wallpaper. (See illustration 137.)

Father's Bookcase

Illustration 135

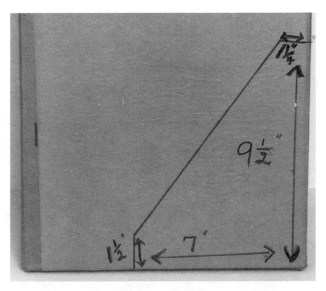

Illustration 136

MATERIALS FOR FATHER'S BOOKCASE

Brush, scissors, corrugated cardboard box, utility knife, wallpaper paste, masking tape, ruler, damp cloth and zebra, cheetah, leopard or tiger designed wallpaper.

DIRECTIONS FOR FATHER'S BOOKCASE

1. Draw side measurement on both sides of box. Draw line across the back 9-1/2" high, joining sides. (See illustration 136.)
2. Cut out with a utility knife.
3. Leave double bottom. Tape seams and edges with masking tape.
4. Cut a piece of wallpaper 20" by 14-1/2" for outside back and bottom. Begin with 1-1/4" overlap at top and ending with same at bottom. Snip corners and overlap edges.
5. Cut a piece for inside back and bottom, 16" long and 13" wide. (It allows for 1/2" overlap on sides.)
6. Lay bookcase on side and trace onto wrong side of wallpaper. Add extra 1/2" to overlap inside. Paste on dotted lines. (See illustration 137.) Do other side likewise.
7. Next, trace the same way for inside, sides. No overlap is necessary.

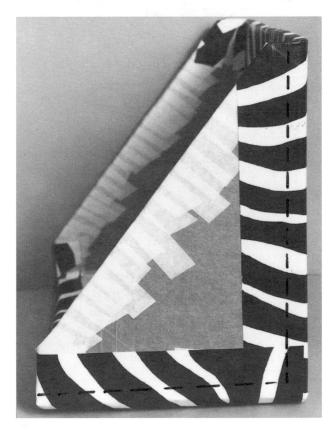

Illustration 137

NOTE

Box used for bookcase is 12" wide. For extra strength, make the bottom double before taping edges.

Letter Box/Paper Clip Dish/Pencil Can

Illustration 138

MATERIALS FOR PAPER CLIP DISH

Ruler, 8 oz. pineapple can, scissors, zebra designed wallpaper (or other animal), brush, black spray paint, glue and compass to make patterns for bottom of cans.

DIRECTIONS FOR PAPER CLIP CAN

1. Remove paper from can. Wash and dry.
2. Spray paint can and dry well.
3. Draw two 3-1/4" circles of wallpaper for bottom of can. (Glue on inside and outside of can.)
4. Next, cut a piece of wallpaper for inside of can 1-7/8" by 10-1/2" and glue on.
5. Last, cut a piece of wallpaper 1-13/16" by 10-3/4" and glue on outside of can.
6. Press down wallpaper again with a damp cloth.

MATERIALS FOR PENCIL CAN

Compass, animal designed wallpaper, brush, scissors, black spray paint, glue, soup can, ruler and damp cloth.

DIRECTIONS FOR PENCIL CAN

1. Remove paper from can, wash and dry.
2. Spray paint inside and top half of can. Let dry, then turn can upside down and paint bottom half.
3. Draw two circles 2-1/2" and glue inside and outside bottom of can.
4. Next, cut a piece of wallpaper 8-1/2" by 3-3/4" and glue inside of can.
5. Then, cut a piece of wallpaper 8-3/4" by 3-3/4" and glue on outside of can.
6. Go over can again with the damp cloth and press out air bubbles.

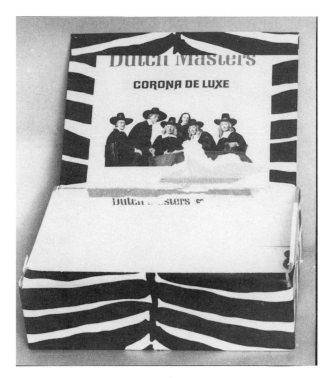

Illustration 139

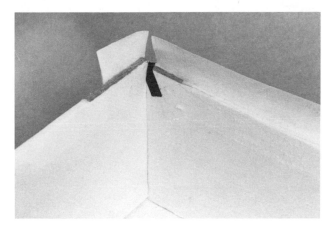

Illustration 140

Notice how corners are cut before gluing down overlap. Glue narrow strip first, then the overlaps.

MATERIALS FOR LETTER BOX

A small knob, vinyl wallpaper, scissors, cigar box, damp cloth, brush, ruler and glue.

DIRECTIONS FOR LETTER BOX

1. Measure a piece of vinyl wallpaper long enough to go around cigar box and overlap 1-1/2" on sides. (See illustration 139.) Snip corner and overlap.
2. Measure box and cut a piece of wallpaper for inside of box.
3. Next cut a piece for side, long enough for both outside and inside of box. Do other side likewise.
4. Drill a hole in center of cover 1/2" from edge and attach knob.
5. If screw for knob is too long, saw it off to fit.

NOTE

Above box is 9-1/2" long, large enough for business letters, along with assorted sizes. Attach a knob for easy opening.

Wastebasket

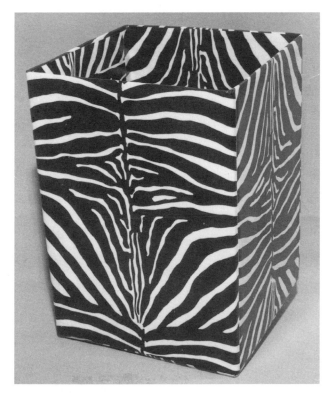

Illustration 141

Illustration 142

Illustration 143

MATERIALS FOR WASTEBASKET

Wallpaper paste, yardstick, a box about 1' square and 17" high, scissors, vinyl wallpaper, brush and a damp cloth.

DIRECTIONS FOR WASTEBASKET

1. Cut a piece of wallpaper 32" by 15".
2. Paste first piece on back, with 1" overlap on top. This piece goes all the way under box, overlapping 1" on all sides. (See illustration 142.)
3. Cut a piece for front 15" wide and 18" long. Overlap 1" at top and sides.
4. Next, cut a piece 13" wide and 30" long. Begin at top overlap of first strip and over inside bottom, overlap sides.
5. Cut two narrow strips 12" by 18-1/2". Glue on the outside, sides.
6. Cut two more 12" by 18-1/2" strips for the inside.

Notice how corners are cut. (Paste narrow strip down first, then the edges.) The outside back and front pieces are pasted on first.

MAKING THE PERFECT GIFT

When you make a gift for someone, choose the type of gift thoughtfully. Is it something the person will use, or do they need it? The expression, "Just what I need!", is thanks enough.

Choosing the wallpaper pattern is also important. Does it signify a hobby or something they enjoy, like nature? Nature is often portrayed in wallpaper designs.

And don't forget the color! If the gift will be part of their home decor, be sure the color coordinates with their color scheme, or your gift may not be displayed. You can create a perfect gift by following these three points.

Bread Knife Shield

Illustration 144

MATERIALS FOR KNIFE SHIELD
Wallpaper with cloth backing, stapler, scissors and marker.

DIRECTIONS FOR KNIFE SHIELD
1. It is imperative that you use wallpaper with cloth backing. It is similar to oilcloth.
2. Trace pattern on wrong side of wallpaper.
3. Cut out, then cut out where indicated on pattern.
4. Fold center on dotted line, and then fold edges on dotted lines as in pattern.
5. Staple edges together, about 1/8" from edge. When done, squeeze the staples flat with pliers.

NOTE
Patterns for Knife Shield and Fish Mobile are on page 68.

Fish Mobile

Illustration 145

MATERIALS FOR FISH MOBILE
Moving eyes, assorted wallpaper, piece of driftwood, small screw eyes, glue, scissors, invisible thread, toothpick, hook screw for hanging, damp cloth and brush.

DIRECTIONS FOR FISH MOBILE
1. Glue pieces of identical wallpaper, back-to-back. Dry overnight under weight.
2. Trace patterns and cut out.
3. Use a toothpick to dab glue on area where you would like the eye to be.
4. Gently press eye on glue. Dry two hours before gluing eye on the other side.
5. Attach screw eyes on bottom of driftwood. Screw in hook screw on top center of driftwood.
6. Use invisible thread to stitch top of fin. Knot and attach other end of thread to screw eye.
7. Make two more fish. Vary lengths of thread from 3-1/2" to 5". Dab glue on knots so they don't come apart.

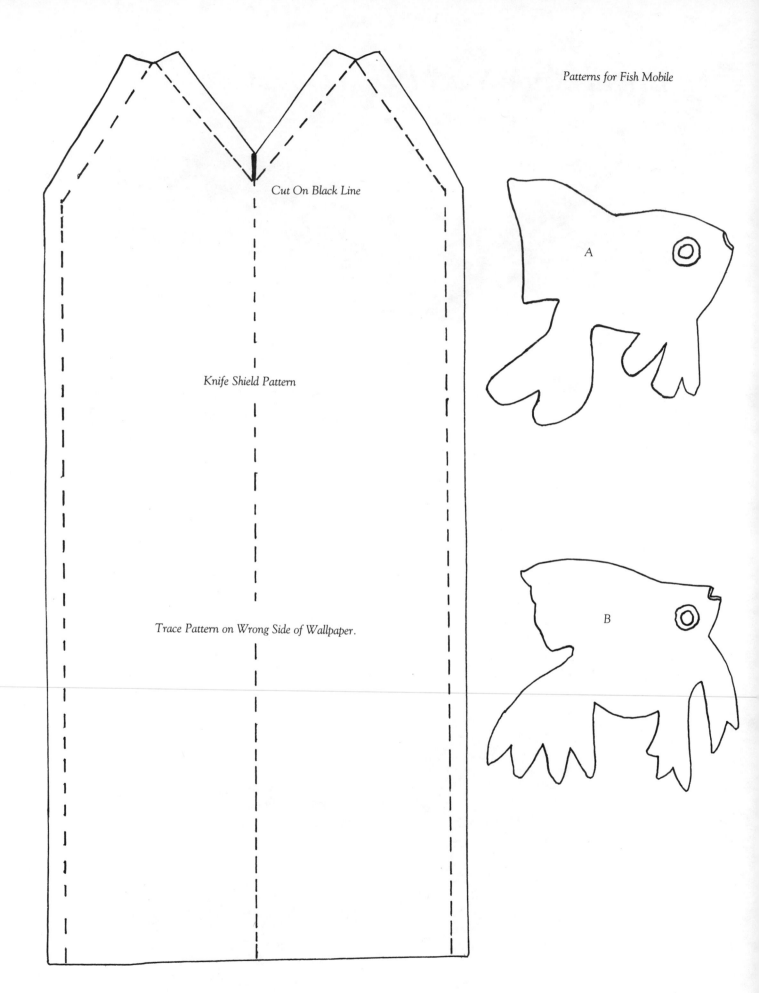

Cut On Black Line

Knife Shield Pattern

Trace Pattern on Wrong Side of Wallpaper.

A

B

Butterfly Mobile

Pumpkin Face Mobile

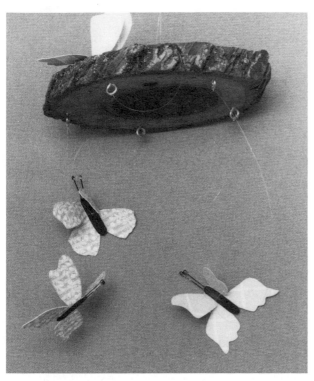

Illustration 146

Illustration 147

MATERIALS FOR BUTTERFLY MOBILE

Wallpaper, glue, invisible thread, scissors, screw eyes, screw hook, 4-1/2" round, stamens for butterfly antennae and damp cloth.

DIRECTIONS FOR BUTTERFLY MOBILE

1. Make butterflies according to directions on page 42, except leave off the magnets.
2. Space screw eyes around bottom of round. Center screw hook on top of round.
3. Stitch center back edge of wing and make a bridge across to other wing (about 1/2"). Tie double knot.
4. Next, tie thread to center of bridge and attach to a screw eye. Dab knots with glue.
5. Make four butterflies. Vary the lengths of thread.

MATERIALS FOR PUMPKIN FACE MOBILE

Glue, driftwood, invisible thread, sponge, scissors, vinyl floor covering, yellow and green wallpaper, screw eyes, screw hook and X-acto knife.

DIRECTIONS FOR PUMPKIN MOBILE

1. Use the pumpkin patterns on page 70. Cut out two of each one — one from the orange wallpaper and another from vinyl floor covering.
2. Glue them together and dry under weight overnight.
3. Cut out eyes and mouth. Make a nose from sponge and paint orange. Glue nose on face.
4. Glue yellow paper behind holes, and an orange pumpkin on back.
5. Glue on green stem.
6. Stitch edge of stem. Knot twice and attach other end to screw eye in driftwood.
7. Make other pumpkins and attach to driftwood. Vary the lengths of thread.
8. Glue vines to driftwood.

Book Jacket

Illustration 148

Illustration 149

MATERIALS FOR BOOK JACKET

Wallpaper, glue, ruler, yardstick, scissors and damp cloth.

DIRECTIONS FOR BOOK JACKET

1. Lay book on wrong side of wallpaper. Hold pages up, leave covers flat. Mark a border of 2-1/4" around book.
2. Cut out pieces even with spine.
3. Next, fold down top, cut corners off and fold over sides.
4. Glue strips of wallpaper across corners and bottom to hold jacket together. Do front cover likewise.

Patterns for Pumpkin Face Mobile

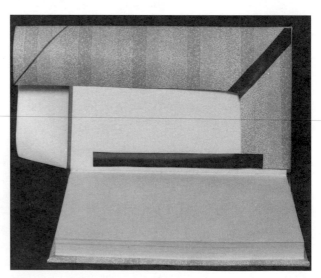

Illustration 150

Portfolio

Illustration 151

Portfolios can be made from most any wallpaper pattern. Choose your colors carefully because they will be a part of your ensemble if used at school or seminars.

Materials for Portfolio
Scissors, wallpaper paste, vinyl wallpaper, yardstick, ruler and damp cloth.

Directions for Portfolio
1. Cut a piece of vinyl wallpaper 19-1/4" wide and 17" long.
2. Then cut a piece of wallpaper, 20-3/8" wide and 17" long.
3. Take the wide piece and draw a line on both sides, 5/8" from edge on the wrong side.
4. Next, apply wallpaper paste to this piece. Center small one on top, using sidelines as a guide.
5. Brush air bubbles and wrinkles out as you do when wallpapering.
6. Place paper towels over wallpaper, then a large board and books. Change damp towels every day until wallpaper feels dry.
7. Cut 4" up the bottom on lines, and cut off strips. (See illustration 152.)
8. Then, turn up the bottom 4" and crease in half the other way.
9. Draw center cutout where crease is (2-3/4" by 1/4"). Place on board and cut out with X-acto knife. (Cutout prevents fold from wrinkling.) Cut only through pocket.
10. Paste down edges and wipe with a damp cloth.
11. Fold and dry under weight.

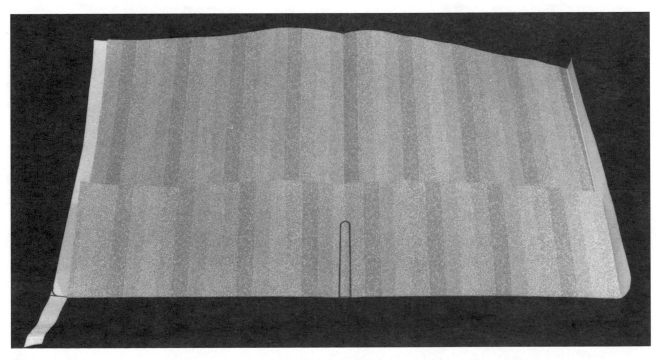

Illustration 152

Open-Faced Recipe Box

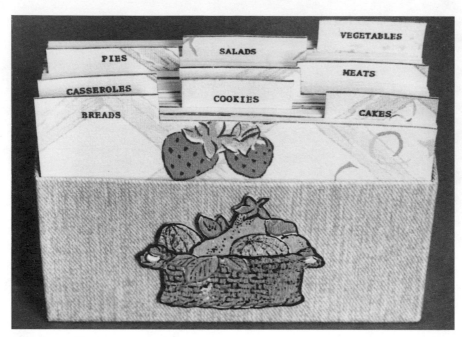

Illustration 153

MATERIALS FOR RECIPE FILE

3" x 5" index cards, vinyl wallpaper, damp cloth, old recipe box, brush, ruler, wallpaper paste, fruit images, piece of Congoleum, tiny brush for outlining and scale model paint.

DIRECTIONS FOR RECIPE FILE

1. Cut off cover of recipe box and remove loose paper. Tape cracks in corners with masking tape.
2. Place box on wallpaper and draw outline. Then mark 3-1/2" beyond outline. (The height of box plus 1/2" for overlapping inside of box.)

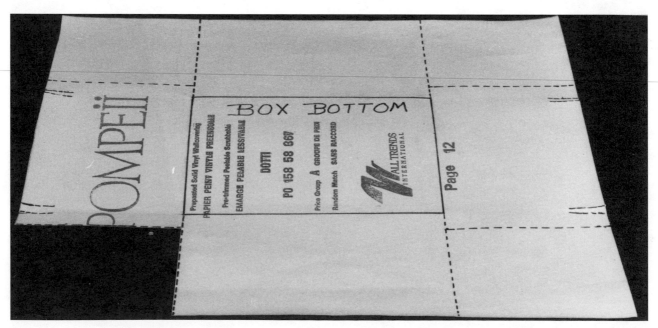

Illustration 154

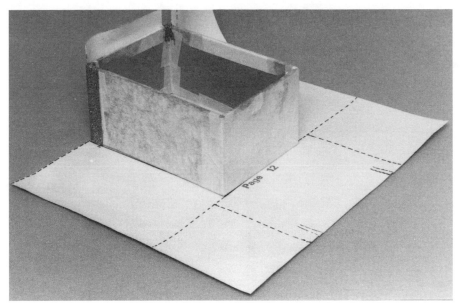

Illustration 155

3. Cut on dotted lines and discard corner pieces. (See illustration 155.)

4. Next, apply paste on wallpaper. Put box on outline and press down.

5. First, bring up ends, overlapping around corners. Snip corners, and glue tabs down.

6. Then fold end down, overlapping inside. Do other end and sides.

7. Cover inside bottom and sides, using outline of box as a pattern.

8. Use index card as a pattern for dividers. (Remember to add tabs.)

9. Cut three tabs of each style: one on left side, middle and right side. You will be using these tabs to identify the different recipe categories.

10. Trace each divider onto wallpaper. Glue together and dry under weight.

11. Trace outline of fruit image on Congoleum. Cut out and glue together. Outline edge of Congoleumwith scale model paint.

12. Glue fruit onto box with undiluted glue. Leave flat until dry.

13. Glue labels onto tabs to identify the recipe categories.

NOTE
Write the labels on tabs with an indelible pen (or type them).

Illustration 156

Coupon Box

Illustration 157

NOTE

Use thin cardboard to make box, and be sure to score it so it bends neatly. Poster board is fine. Mat board will work for dividers.

MATERIALS FOR COUPON BOX

Utility knife, vinyl wallpaper, Styrofoam 5/8" thick to make back filler, ruler, 1/8" thick cardboard for dividers, poster board for box, scissors, paper clips, damp cloth and glue.

DIRECTIONS FOR COUPON BOX

1. Draw an outline of box bottom, 3-1/2" by 7".
2. Next, mark off 3-1/2" on all sides of outline. (See illustration 158.)
3. Then, cut on dotted lines where indicated in illustration 158.
4. Score on solid lines and across corners.
5. Now, fold up ends and bring up sides, overlapping around ends.
6. Brush glue on end overlaps. Put clips on corners until glue sets.
7. The ends have double overlaps, but you must reinforce the sides. Glue a piece of tablet cardboard on the sides, inside the box.

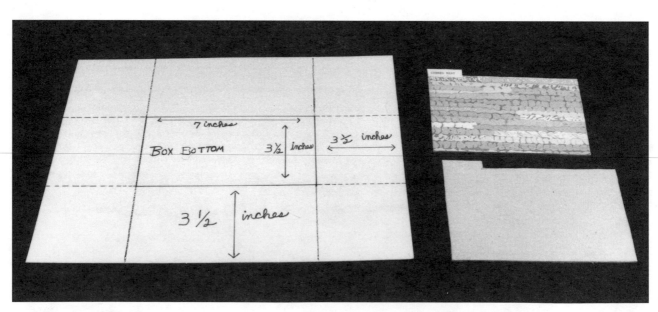

Illustration 158

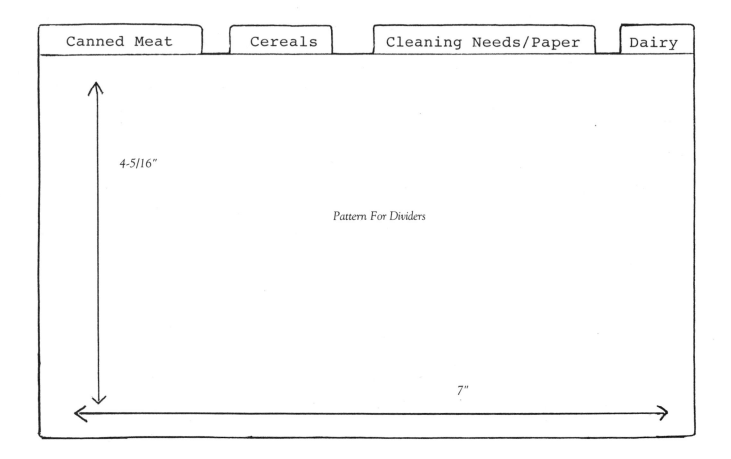

Canned Meat   Cereals   Cleaning Needs/Paper   Dairy

4-5/16"

Pattern For Dividers

7"

MATERIALS FOR COUPON BOX DIVIDERS

Mat board, utility knife, wallpaper, damp cloth, ruler and glue.

DIRECTIONS FOR DIVIDERS

1. Trace above four patterns onto mat board. (Make three from each pattern.)
2. Next, place mat board on a board and carefully cut out the dividers with a utility knife.
3. Cut out duplicates of each divider from wallpaper and glue together. Dry overnight under weight.
4. Type labels and glue onto tabs. Arrange in alphabetical order.

NOTE

If you ask, a picture framing store may give you scrap pieces of mat board to make the dividers.

MATERIALS FOR COVERING BOX

Ruler, wallpaper paste, vinyl wallpaper, scissors, darker wallpaper to make the label COUPONS, yardstick, damp cloth and glue.

DIRECTIONS FOR COVERING BOX

1. Draw an outline of box on wrong side of wallpaper. (See illustration 155.)
2. Next draw a 4" line beyond this line on all sides. This allows for 1/2" overlap to inside.
3. Complete box by following steps 3-6 of Recipe File on page 73.
4. Next, cover a 5/8" thick piece of plywood or Styrofoam with matching wallpaper. This is used as a filler if you have only a few coupons.
5. Arrange dividers in box.
6. Cut out contrasting letters for COUPONS and glue on front of box.

Purse Stiffeners

Illustration 159

Have you ever had a purse that was so limp that it had no shape? Just put in a stiffener. If you make if from silk wallpaper, it will look like the lining of the purse.

MATERIALS FOR STIFFENER

Scissors, corrugated cardboard, silk wallpaper, glue and damp cloth.

DIRECTIONS FOR PURSE STIFFENER

1. Draw an outline of the purse on the cardboard.
2. Next, trim off cardboard so it fits inside of purse.
3. Trace a duplicate of this cardboard shape on wallpaper.
4. Trace another one, 1/2" larger.
5. Glue larger one onto cardboard first, overlapping to back. Then, glue other piece of wallpaper onto back of cardboard.
6. Dry overnight under weight.

Mirror Frame

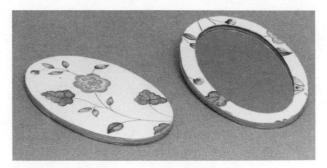

Illustration 160

DIRECTIONS FOR MIRROR FRAME

1. Draw two outlines of mirror on thin cardboard, and two more onto vinyl wallpaper.
2. Glue the wallpaper outlines on the cardboard ones. Dry overnight.
3. Glue one on back of mirror.
4. Next, outline a 1/4" border on the other wallpaper. Cut out center.
5. Glue frame on front of mirror.
6. Optional: Paint edge of mirror.

Underliner Guide

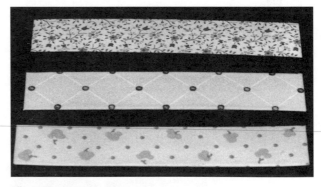

Illustration 161

DIRECTIONS FOR UNDERLINER

1. Cut a piece of plastic 1" by 5" from a large Cool Whip cover.
2. Next, cut a piece of wallpaper 1-1/2" by 5-1/2". Glue on plastic, overlapping back.
3. Glue a smaller piece on back to cover rest of plastic.

Tasseled Bookmark

Illustration 162

MATERIALS FOR BOOKMARK

Baby yarn, brush, scissors, paper punch, thin cardboard, glue and damp cloth.

DIRECTIONS FOR TASSELED BOOKMARK

1. Trace the pattern onto a large Cool Whip cover.
2. Center pattern over a wallpaper design and outline.
3. Next, cut out and glue on cardboard. Dry overnight under weight.
4. Cut out bookmarks and punch out small hole in top. Tie on tassel.

*Pattern
for
Tasseled
Bookmark*

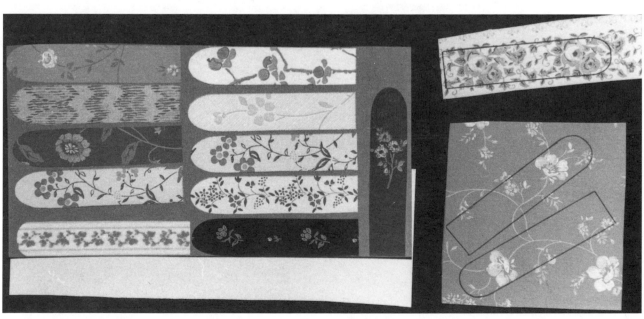

Illustration 163

3-D Butterfly Gift Box

Illustration 164

MATERIALS FOR 3-D BUTTERFLY BOX

Wallpaper paste, ruler, wallpaper with butterfly images, flower stamens for butterfly antennae, glue, scissors, magnetic tape and a 5 lb. candy box with cover.

DIRECTIONS FOR WALLPAPER
MAGNETIC BUTTERFLIES

1. Cut a circle around a wallpaper butterfly and glue it back-to-back to a piece of same designed wallpaper. (See illustration 165.)
2. When dry, cut out butterfly.
3. Cut out two black bodies (from black wallpaper) to fit your butterfly. Glue one on top.
4. Glue antennae behind the head.
5. Carefully, glue other body over antennae. (See illustration 93.)
6. Glue small magnet on butterfly.

DIRECTIONS FOR COVERING BOX

1. Place box on wallpaper and draw outline of bottom.
2. Measure height of box and add 1/2" for overlap to inside. (Example: Box is 2-1/4" high. Add 1/2" for overlap inside. [2-1/4" + 1/2" = 2-3/4"] Draw a line 2-3/4" beyond box outline.)
3. Draw line across ends. Cut end lines up to box. (See illustration 165.)
4. Apply paste to wallpaper. Place box on outline. Fold up ends and overlap to inside.
5. Next, paste down side and overlap to inside.
6. Follow steps 1-5 for the cover.
7. Let box dry overnight.
8. Use undiluted glue to glue tiny magnets on cover wherever you want a magnetic butterfly. (Use larger magnets if your butterfly is big.)
9. Tie ribbon around box, then add the magnetic butterflies.

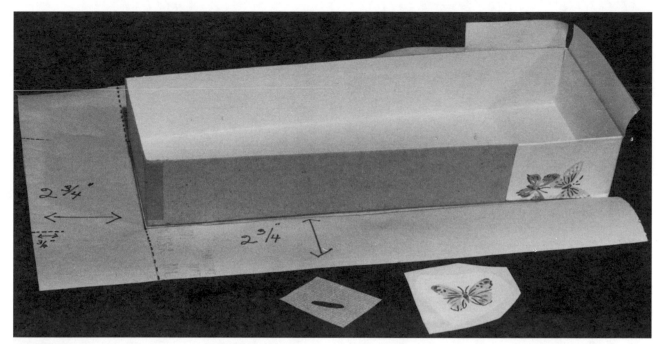

Illustration 165

Even though wallpaper designs keep changing, most likely you will be able to find one with butterflies.

Illustration 166

MATERIALS FOR 3-D FLOWER GIFT BOX

Shoe box, scissors, Congoleum, ruler, vinyl floral wallpaper, glue and wallpaper paste. (Use glue for flowers and paste to cover box.)

3-D Floral Gift Box

Illustration 167

DIRECTIONS FOR 3-D FLORAL GIFT BOX

1. Follow steps 1-5 of "Directions for Covering Box" on page 78.
2. Next, cut out wallpaper flowers and glue on Congoleum. Make enough for cover and sides of box.
3. Dry under weight.
4. Cut out flowers and glue over their matching floral shapes on the cover. (Use undiluted glue.)
5. Do one side and wait until glue sets before doing another side.

Flower Cards/Tags

Silk Gift Box

Illustration 168

MATERIALS FOR GIFT CARDS AND TAGS

Pinking shears, ribbon, scissors, thin cardboard, front view wallpaper flowers, ruler, glue, stapler and damp cloth.

DIRECTIONS FOR FLOWER CARDS

1. Cut out wallpaper flower.
2. Score and fold a piece of cardboard to fit flower. (See illustration 168.)
3. Apply glue to flower and place on fold. Use a damp cloth to press down firmly.
4. Let dry overnight under weight.
5. Cut around flower, except between top area.
6. Write verse and names inside.
7. Staple backside to ribbon.

DIRECTIONS FOR SMALL DOUBLE CARDS

1. Score and fold a piece of cardboard. Then, cut a 2-3/8" by 3" section from the folded cardboard.
2. Then, cut a piece of wallpaper (with flower image) the same size.
3. Trim edge with pinking shears. Glue to cardboard. (See illustration 168.)
4. Write names inside.

Illustration 169

DIRECTIONS FOR GIFT TAG

1. Cut out wallpaper flower or any other wallpaper image.
2. Glue onto cardboard. Dry under weight overnight.
3. Cut out card. Punch out a small hole near top for ribbon.
4. Write names on back.

DIRECTIONS FOR COVERING GIFT BOX

1. Use silk wallpaper if possible.
2. Follow steps 1-5 of "Directions for Covering Box" on page 78.
3. Tie on ribbon and attach card.

NOTE

Try to get an outdated silk wallpaper catalog. They have lots of coordinating colors.

Gift Boxes/Tags

Illustration 170

DIRECTIONS FOR WRAPPING A BOX

1. Wrap it the same way as you would when using gift wrap. Tape ends.
2. Example: The box in illustration 170 (one with duck tag) is wallpaper wrapped.
3. Glue or staple tag to ribbon.

DIRECTIONS FOR NATURE GIFT BOX

1. Choose a wallpaper design that pertains to the hobby of the person receiving it.
2. Follow steps 1-5 of "Directions for Covering Box" on page 78.
3. Let dry overnight before boxing gift.
4. Tie ribbon around box, leaving enough ends to attach card.

REFACING A USED BOX

If the box is like new, just redo the cover.

Use wallpaper with the same color background as the bottom of box.

DIRECTIONS FOR OVAL GIFT TAG

1. Make a see-through pattern from a large Cool Whip cover.
2. Next, center pattern over wallpaper image and outline.
3. Cut out and glue on thin cardboard. Dry under weight overnight.
4. Punch out a small hole near the top to attach ribbon.
5. Paint edge of tag to match ribbon. Write names on back of tag.

DIRECTIONS FOR CUT-OUT GIFT TAG

1. Cut out a wallpaper image that matches the box you will be attaching it to.
2. Glue it on thin cardboard, then dry overnight under weight.
3. Cut out image and write name on back.
4. Glue or staple tag to ribbon.

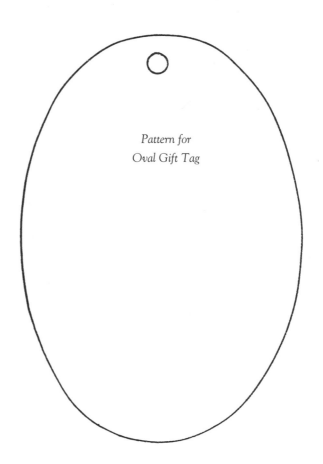

Pattern for Oval Gift Tag

Lined Envelopes/Flower Note Paper

Illustration 171

MATERIALS FOR LINED ENVELOPES
Ruler, thinned glue, silk wallpaper, drawing paper and scissors.

DIRECTIONS FOR LINED ENVELOPES
1. Trace envelope pattern on drawing paper and cut out. (See page 84.)
2. Cut out liner from wallpaper.
3. Apply glue sparingly around the edge of liner, and glue on top of envelope. (See illustration 172.)
4. Crease on dotted lines.
5. Fold side flaps over first. Now fold up bottom flap and apply glue on edges where arrows indicate.
6. Wipe with damp cloth. Dry overnight under weight.
7. Glue edge of top flap on envelope (indicated by arrows).
8. Leave flat until dry.
9. Moisten top flap to seal like purchased envelope.

NOTE
Silk wallpaper is great for lined envelopes. If you use a catalog, use a corner without print. If any print remains, blot it out with liquid paper.

MATERIALS FOR FLOWER NOTE PAPER
Drawing paper, wallpaper flowers, small brush, scissors, damp cloth and glue.

DIRECTIONS FOR FLOWER NOTE PAPER
1. Cut a 5-7/8" by 7-5/8" sheet of drawing paper and fold in half lengthwise.
2. Cut out a small wallpaper flower that matches liner of envelope.
3. Glue flower to upper right-hand corner. Wipe with a damp cloth.
4. Next, place napkin over flower and dry overnight under weight.

Illustration 172

Semilined Envelope/Trimmed Note Paper

Illustration 173

MATERIALS FOR SEMILINED ENVELOPE

Thinned glue, silk wallpaper, ruler, scissors, small brush, drawing paper and damp cloth.

DIRECTIONS FOR SEMILINED ENVELOPE

1. Trace envelope pattern (on page 84) on drawing paper and cut out.
2. Cut out semiliner from wallpaper. Apply glue where indicated by arrows and glue to envelope back.
3. Fold and crease sides and bottom flap.
4. Glue bottom flap where indicated by arrows.
5. Place paper towel over envelope and dry overnight under weight.

DIRECTIONS FOR TRIMMED NOTE PAPER

1. Follow the same directions for Flower Note Paper, but use a side trim instead of a flower.

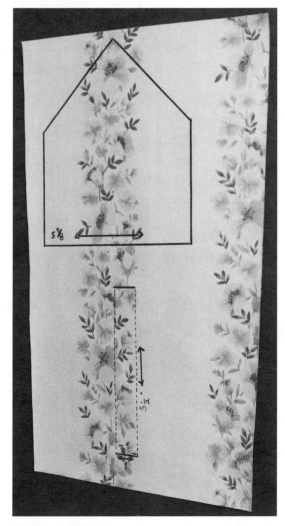

Illustration 174

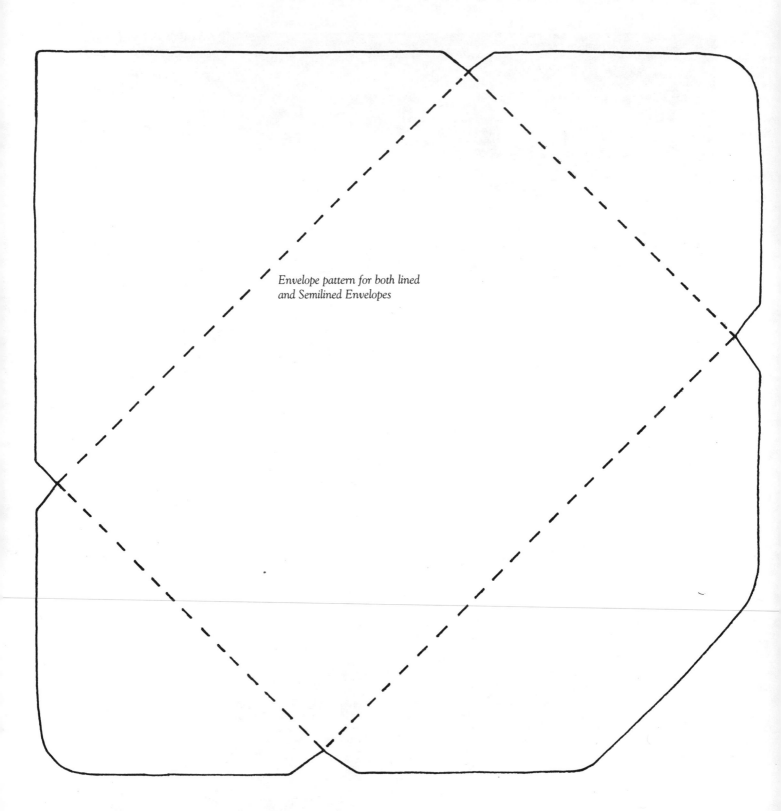

Envelope pattern for both lined and Semilined Envelopes

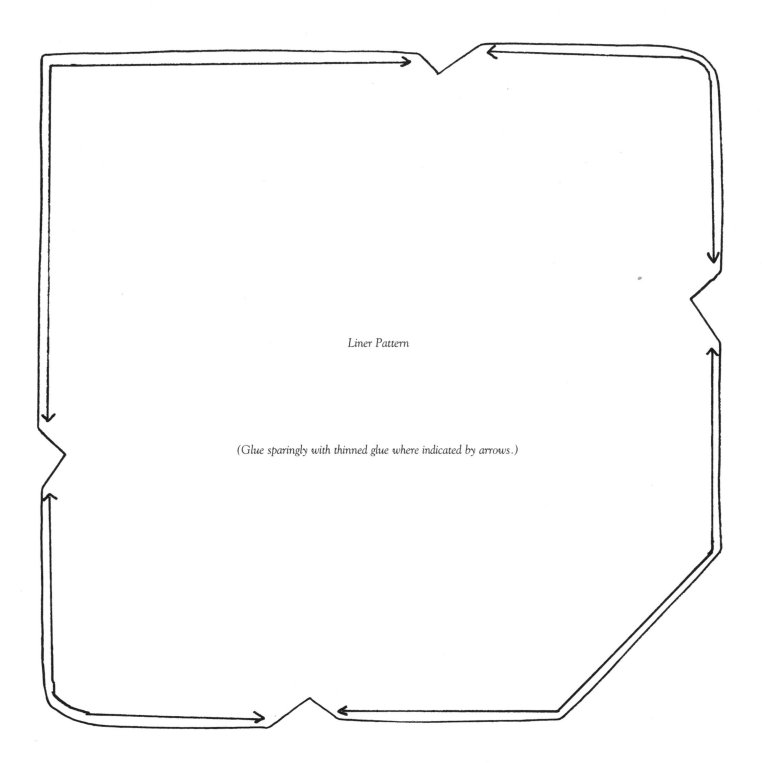

Liner Pattern

(Glue sparingly with thinned glue where indicated by arrows.)

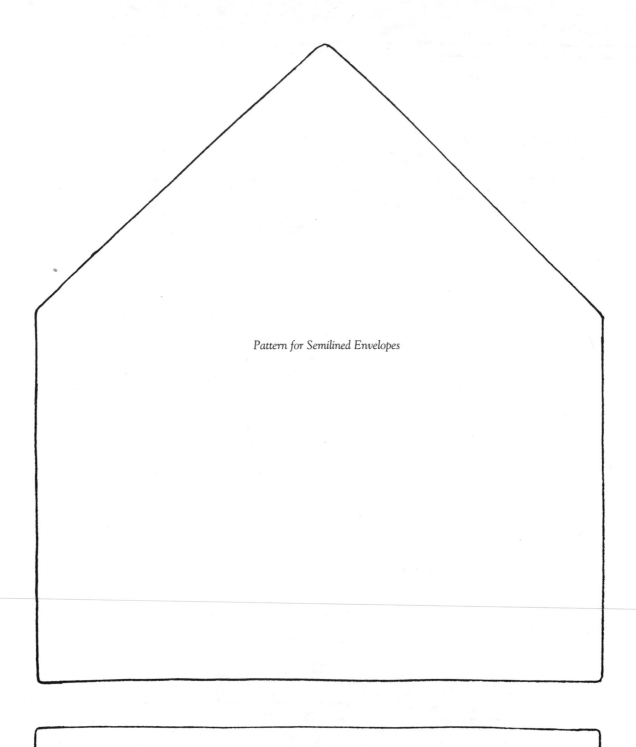

Pattern for Semilined Envelopes

Trim pattern for Note Paper
(Cut edges with pinking shears.)

Refacing Binders

Illustration 175

Illustration 176

If logo spreads over a large area on cover and spine of binder, cover the full length with wallpaper.

If logo covers a small space, cover it with wallpaper. Add your own logo in wallpaper letters.

Sheet Lifters

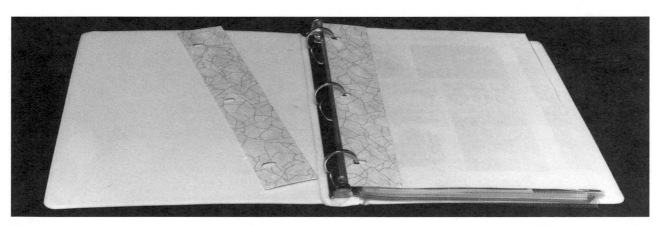

Illustration 177

MATERIALS FOR SHEET LIFTERS
Mat board, thinned glue, scissors, ruler, vinyl wallpaper, large paper punch and a damp cloth.

DIRECTIONS FOR SHEET LIFTERS
1. Cut two pieces of mat board 2" by 11".
2. Next cut a piece of vinyl wallpaper 2-1/2" by 9".
3. Center mat board on glued wallpaper. Fold over ends. Then, snip corners and glue sides. Dry overnight under weight.
4. Use notebook paper as a pattern and punch out three holes in mat.
5. Cut a piece of wallpaper 10-7/8" by 1-7/8" and glue on back. Let dry.
6. Punch holes through back piece.

NOTE
Get scraps of mat board from a frame shop or use cardboard.

Stationery

Illustration 178

If you have a stationery box about 5" by 9", cover it with matching wallpaper instead of making a new one. Adjust size of stationery to fit the box.

MATERIALS FOR STATIONERY
Drawing paper, pinking shears, wallpaper, scissors, wallcovering paste and damp cloth.

DIRECTIONS FOR STATIONERY
1. Make a cardboard pattern 4-1/2" by 8". Cut out a facsimile from wallpaper and drawing paper.
2. Using a pinking shears, cut a border around wallpaper and paste it onto the drawing paper.
3. Place between paper towels in a telephone book and dry overnight.
4. Score and fold on dotted lines. (See illustration 179.)
5. Make a 1" band from drawing paper and put around notes.
6. Make twelve notes to a set.

DIRECTIONS FOR ENVELOPES
1. Trace envelope pattern (on page 89) on drawing paper and cut out.
2. Crease on dotted lines.
3. Fold over sides, then glue bottom flap on top of sides.
4. Put a thin coat of glue on edge of top flap and dry flat.
5. Moisten glue to seal, like you would on a boughten envelope.
6. Make twelve envelopes to a set. Then, band the envelopes.

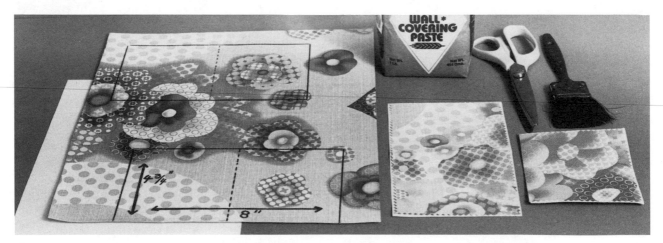

Illustration 179

Choose wallpaper with an interesting composition. Use wallcovering paste for notes and covering box.

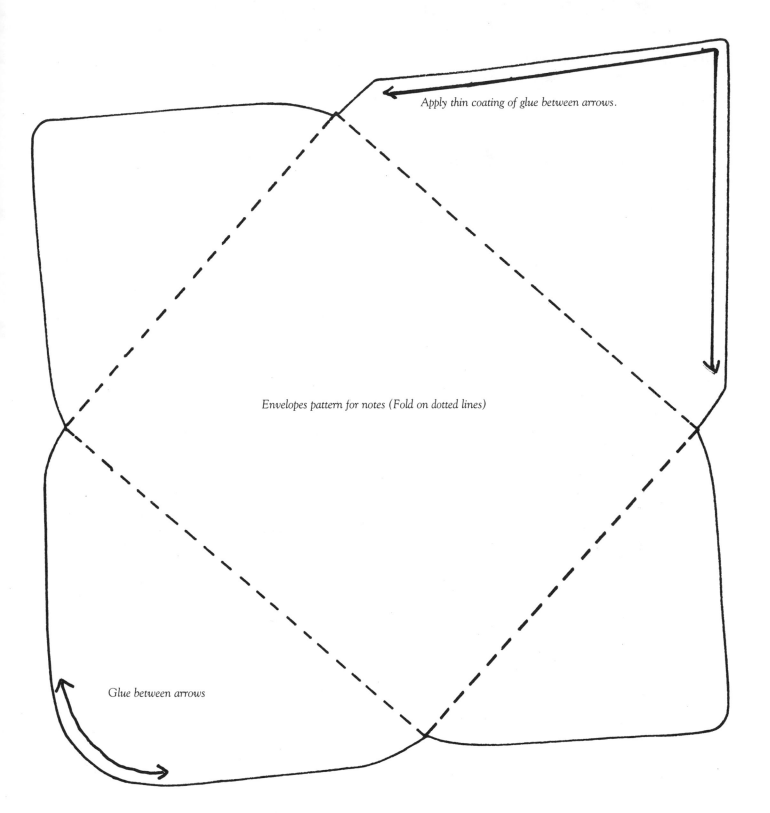

Apply thin coating of glue between arrows.

Envelopes pattern for notes (Fold on dotted lines)

Glue between arrows

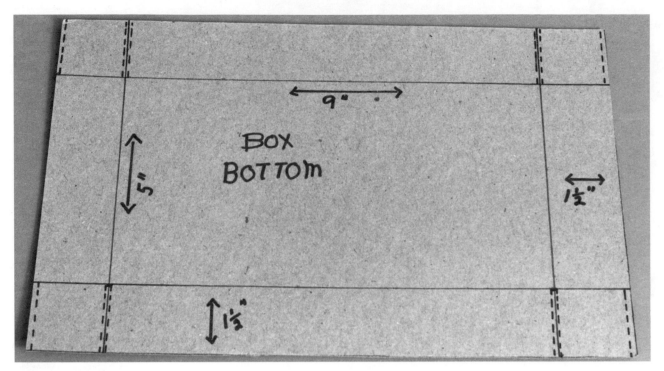

Illustration 180

MATERIALS FOR BOX

Large used box, ruler, scissors, damp cloth, paper clips and wallpaper.

DIRECTIONS FOR BOX BOTTOM

1. Cut a rectangle 8" by 12" from the side of box.
2. Draw a 1-1/2" line around edge of rectangle. (See illustration 180.)
3. Cut out slit of cardboard where indicated by dotted lines.
4. Score on lines with dull knife, using ruler as a guide. Fold up ends and sides. Bend tabs.
5. Apply undiluted glue to outside of tabs. Hold sides over tabs with paper clips until glue has set.

NOTE

The cover is larger than the bottom so that it slides smoothly over the bottom box. The cardboard strips glued around the bottom of the cover keep it from going way on. Therefore it is easy to remove. It also adds height to box.

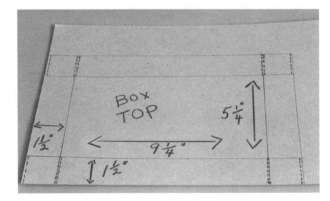

Illustration 181

DIRECTIONS FOR BOX COVER

1. Cut a rectangle 8-1/4" by 12-1/4".
2. Draw a 1-1/2" line around edge of rectangle for sides. (See illustration 181.)
3. Cut out slit of cardboard where indicated by dotted lines.
4. Score on solid lines with dull knife, using ruler as a guide.
5. Fold ends and sides.
6. Apply undiluted glue to outside of tabs. Press side over tabs. Put paper clips on corners until dry.
7. Cut two strips of cardboard 3/4" by 9-1/8", and two strips 3/4" by 5-1/8".
8. Glue strips around bottom sides of cover. (See illustration 182.)

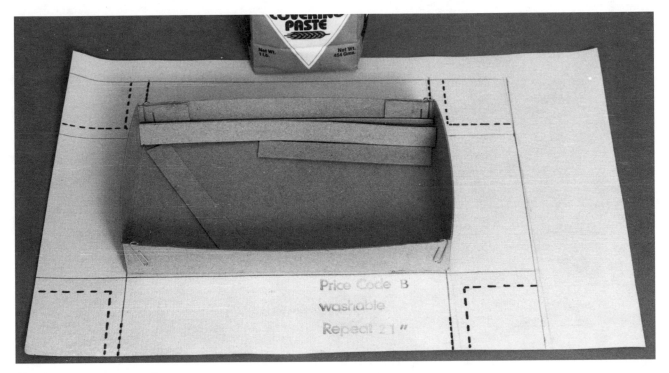

Illustration 182   Box Cover

DIRECTIONS FOR COVERING BOX COVER

1. Lay box cover on the wrong side of wallpaper and outline.
2. Draw a line 2-1/2" beyond box outline.
3. Cut corners where indicated by dotted lines. (illustration 182)
4. Apply paste to wallpaper. Place box on outline and bring up sides, overlapping to inside of box. Fold corners and bring up ends. Add extra glue to corners.

COVERING BOX BOTTOM

Follow the same directions to cover box bottom as for cover.

MATERIALS FOR FALSE BOTTOM

Poster board, ruler, tablet cardboard for center support and scoring knife.

DIRECTIONS FOR FALSE BOTTOM

1. Cut a piece of tablet cardboard 5" by 5" for false bottom support.
2. Draw a line 3/4" from edge on opposite sides. Score and bend.
3. Reinforce support legs with an extra thickness of cardboard.

Illustration 183   Box Bottom

4. Place support in center of box. (See illustration 183.)
5. Cut a piece of poster board 4-7/8" by 10-1/4" for false bottom.
6. Mark a line on each end 3/4" from edge. Score on line and bend.
7. Reinforce legs with a strip of cardboard.
8. Place false bottom over middle support.
9. Place notes and envelopes over false bottom.
10. Make a divider to put between notes and envelopes.

Greeting Cards

Illustration 184

MATERIALS FOR CARDS AND NOTES
1-1/2" brush, drawing paper, heavy typing paper, glue for envelopes, wallpaper paste for cards, ruler, scissors and damp cloth.

DIRECTIONS FOR GREETING CARDS
1. Make a pattern of a rectangle 4-1/2" by 9".

2. Trace one each of wallpaper and poster board.
3. Paste wallpaper on poster board and dry between paper towels in a telephone book. Dry overnight, then replace damp towels with dry ones. Dry one more day.
4. Score and fold. Write greetings inside.

Note Cards

Illustration 185

DIRECTIONS FOR NOTES
1. Trace one each of wallpaper and heavy typing paper.
2. Paste wallpaper onto typing paper and dry between paper towels in a telephone book for two days.
3. Fold on dotted line as shown in illustration 186.

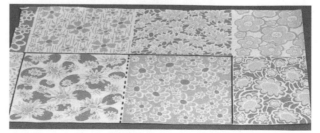

Illustration 186

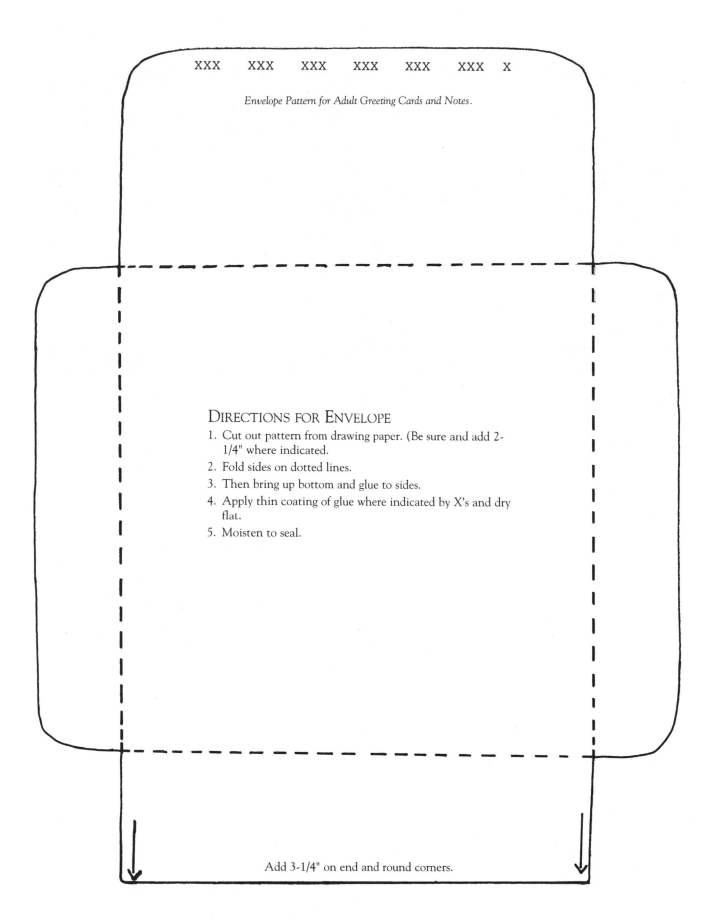

Envelope Pattern for Adult Greeting Cards and Notes.

XXX   XXX   XXX   XXX   XXX   XXX   X

DIRECTIONS FOR ENVELOPE

1. Cut out pattern from drawing paper. (Be sure and add 2-1/4" where indicated.
2. Fold sides on dotted lines.
3. Then bring up bottom and glue to sides.
4. Apply thin coating of glue where indicated by X's and dry flat.
5. Moisten to seal.

Add 3-1/4" on end and round corners.

Nature Greeting Cards

Illustration 187

NATURE GREETING CARDS

Follow the directions for Floral Greeting Cards, except use wallpaper nature scenes.

MATERIALS FOR VALENTINE CARDS

Pink poster board, red wallpaper, permanent marker, glue, scissors, red glitter, ribbon and toothpick.

DIRECTIONS FOR HEART BOUQUET CARD

1. Cut out a piece of pink poster board 4" by 7-1/2".
2. Score and fold in half.
3. Cut out hearts from red wallpaper and glue to cardboard.
4. Draw stems and leaves.
5. Poke two small holes by stem to thread ribbon through. Tie ribbon.
6. Use toothpick to outline hearts with glue. Shake glitter over glue and let dry. Write in "Be my valentine" or a similar phrase.

DIRECTIONS FOR TWIN HEARTS CARD

Follow above directions through 2. Then, cut out two large hearts and glue to cardboard. See photo. Outline hearts with glue and shake on glitter. Let dry. Write in "Yours Truly" or similar phrase.

Twin Hearts/ Heart Bouquet

Illustration 188

Pattern for Twin Hearts Card

Pattern for Heart Bouquet Card

Doily Valentines

Illustration 189

Illustration 190

MATERIALS FOR DOILY VALENTINES

Red or white paper doilies, wallpaper, brush, thin cardboard, damp cloth, scissors and thinned glue.

DIRECTIONS FOR DOILY VALENTINES

1. Fold a 6-1/2" by 13" piece of thin cardboard in half.
2. Apply thinned glue to doily and place on fold of cardboard.
3. Pat doily with a damp cloth and wipe off all glue.
4. Place between paper towels in a telephone book until dry.
5. Cut out valentine. (Do not cut around part of heart that touches fold.)
6. Use pattern to cut out a wallpaper design that you like. Glue on center of doily. Dry overnight.
7. Write a verse inside of valentine. Use calligraphy if possible.

NOTE

There are numerous wallpaper designs that have hearts on them, so check the outdated catalogs.

*Envelope pattern is on page 96.

Pattern for Doily Valentine

Pattern for Valentine Envelope

Place this side on fold

DIRECTIONS FOR VALENTINE ENVELOPE

1. Make envelope pattern by tracing this pattern on fold of paper. Unfold pattern and trace on poster board.
2. Draw pattern on sheet of drawing paper and cut out.
3. Fold sides where indicated by dotted line.
4. Glue sparingly between arrows and press down back.
5. Fold bottom tab and glue over back of envelope.
6. Crease down top flap.

Fold on dotted lines.

Wooden Kitchen Plaques

Illustration 191

Miniature Frames

Illustration 193

DIRECTIONS FOR WOODEN PLAQUE

1. Cut two or three pieces of wood 4-1/2" by 6", from a 1" thick board.
2. Bevel edges and sand smooth.
3. Next, stain or paint the plaque to match your kitchen cabinets.
4. Cut out wallpaper images 3-1/2" by 5" from the same roll that you used on your wall, and glue on plaques.
5. Attach hanger and hang side by side on wall. (2" apart)

DIRECTIONS FOR MINIATURE FRAMES

1. Cut a piece of corrugated cardboard the size of your frame.
2. Cut a wallpaper design (size of frame) from the same roll that was used on your wall.
3. Glue design onto the cardboard.
4. Frame. (no need for glass)
5. Attach screw eyes and wire for hanger.
6. Complete other frames likewise.

Wooden Plate Decor

Illustration 192

DIRECTIONS FOR WOODEN PLATE DECOR

1. Stain wooden plate to match the kitchen cabinets.
2. Cut out a wallpaper image from the pattern used on your wall and glue onto plate.
3. Wipe off excess glue with damp cloth.
4. Attach hanger to back of plate.

Drawer Liners

DIRECTIONS FOR DRAWER LINERS

1. Use leftover wallpaper from your walls.
2. To clean, just wipe with a damp cloth.

Switch Cover

Illustration 194

Illustration 197

MATERIALS FOR SWITCH COVERS

Glue, Congoleum, wallpaper and scissors.

DIRECTIONS FOR SWITCH COVER

1. Remove switch cover and use as a pattern. Now cut a piece of wallpaper matching the one cut out for switch cover. (illustration 194)
2. Next, trace cover on Congoleum. (See illustration 197.)
3. Glue wallpaper on Congoleum and dry overnight under weight.
4. Outline wallpaper with indelible felt pen. (use ruler). Let dry and punch holes for screws.
5. *Put switch cover in place*, then place wallpaper cover over and put the screws through both covers.

Spoon and Fork/Plaster Plaque

Illustration 195

Illustration 196

DIRECTIONS FOR SPOON AND FORK

1. Glue a wallpaper image matching your wallpaper onto a wooden fork and spoon.
2. Drill a tiny hole in the top of handle and hang on headless nail.

DIRECTIONS FOR PLASTER PLAQUE

1. Mix plaster according to directions and pour into mold. When the plaster begins to set, push end of a wire loop into plaster for hanger.
2. Let set until hard. Remove from mold and let dry out for one week.
3. Paint plaque the dominant color in your wallpaper. Let dry.
4. Lay plaque on wallpaper design and trace around it.
5. Trim design to fit plaque.
6. Glue design on plaque.

Child's First Puzzle

Illustration 198

MATERIALS FOR CHILD'S PUZZLE

Ruler, wallpaper animal image, X-acto knife, white vinyl wallpaper, 1-1/2" brush for gluing, Congoleum, glue, scissors, cutting board, Masonite, scale model paint, small brush for outlining and a damp cloth.

DIRECTIONS FOR CHILD'S PUZZLE

1. Cut a 9-1/2" by 12" piece each of Masonite, Congoleum, and white vinyl wallpaper.

2. Apply glue to the wrong side of Congoleum. Place wallpaper on top. Press down with a damp cloth. Use a sweeping motion until air pockets are all out.

3. Glue image in center of wallpaper. Dry overnight under weight.

4. Then place on board and cut out image with an X-acto knife.

5. Trim edge of image with a scissors until it fits inside of frame. Paint the edges of image and stencil black. (See illustration 198.) Be sure to wipe off excess paint while wet.

6. Glue the stencil to smooth side of Masonite. Dry under weight.

7. Paint 1/4" border around frame.

8. Draw puzzle pattern on image.

9. Place image on a cutting board and cut out with an X-acto knife.

10. Trim, then glaze cut edges of puzzle with thinned glue.

NOTE

Choose a large wallpaper animal image with a simple outline. This is a child's first puzzle, so cut large pieces. Use a ruler when you draw the puzzle pieces so that they fit smoothly. After the child outgrows it, cut the bigger pieces in two. Glaze the newly cut edges with thinned glue. Wipe off excess glue with a damp cloth.

Illustration 199

NOTE

This child's puzzle will survive a family of siblings if you adhere to the directions. Glazing the cut edges of the puzzle prevents the wallpaper and Congoleum from separating. Painting the outside edge serves the same purpose, besides giving it a professional, finished look.

Illustration 200

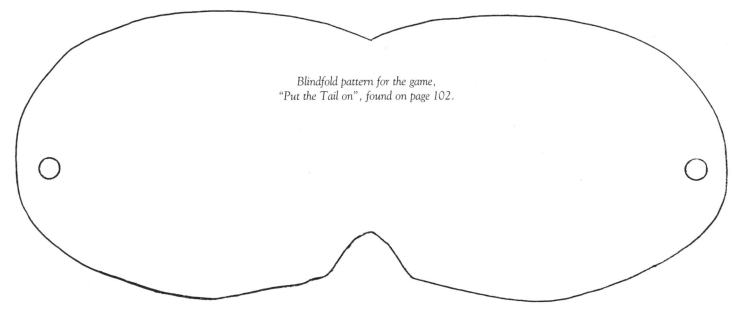

*Blindfold pattern for the game,
"Put the Tail on", found on page 102.*

Match the Tails

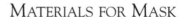

Illustration 201

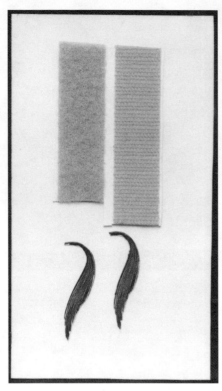

Illustration 202

MATERIALS FOR MASK

Heavy wrapping string, glue, vinyl wallpaper, paper punch and scissors.

DIRECTIONS FOR MASK

1. Glue two pieces of vinyl wallpaper back-to-back. Dry overnight under weight.
2. Draw pattern onto wallpaper and cut out.
3. Punch out holes for string and attach a 24" string to each side.

OBJECT OF GAME

The blindfolded child who matches the most tails wins.

MATERIALS FOR "MATCH THE TAILS"

Wallpaper with animal images, damp cloth, scissors, Velcro, wallpaper for edge trimming, yardstick, piece of plywood 24" by 26", brush, glue and white enamel paint.

DIRECTIONS FOR "MATCH THE TAILS"

1. Spray paint board. Let dry.
2. Cut out animals and glue onto board. Dry under weight.
3. Cut out an identical tail for each animal from the same wallpaper. Glue tails to thin cardboard and dry overnight under weight.
4. Cut out and glue a small piece of fuzzy Velcro on back of tails.
5. Glue the other side of Velcro on tail of the animals on the board.
6. Glue a 1" trim of vinyl wallpaper around edge of board. Wipe off excess glue with a damp cloth.

Checkerboard

Illustration 203

Illustration 204

MATERIALS FOR CHECKERBOARD

A red and black piece of vinyl wallpaper, 13-1/2" square piece of Masonite, scissors, yardstick, light wallpaper, brush, glue and damp cloth.

DIRECTIONS FOR CHECKERBOARD

1. Cut a 13-1/2" square of Masonite.
2. Mark off 3/4" border around edge of Masonite.
3. Next, mark every 1-1/2" all around inside of border. (See illustration 204.)
4. Then with ruler, connect marks across board.
   Turn board and connect lines on this side to form a checkerboard pattern. You now have sixty-four 1-1/2" squares.
5. On the wrong side of wallpaper, measure off thirty-two black and thirty-two red 1-1/2" squares.
6. Glue alternating colors on board. (See illustration 204.)
7. Glue a 3/4" wide strip of black wallpaper around border of board.
8. Then, glue a 3/16" strip of light wallpaper on inside edge of border.

Box for Marbles

Illustration 205

MATERIALS FOR MARBLE BOX

Tin box that is about 4-1/2" by 4-1/2" (3" high), small knob, wallpaper images, glue and scissors.

DIRECTIONS FOR MARBLE BOX

1. Cut out wallpaper images that a child would like and glue them on box.
2. Drill a hole in center of cover for screw.
3. Attach knob. (Put a washer under the head of screw.)

Silly Goose Game

Illustration 206

MATERIALS FOR SILLY GOOSE GAME

Wallpaper animal images, wallpaper paste, indelible black pen, ruler, poster board, brush, vinyl wallpaper, scissors, glue and damp cloth.

DIRECTIONS FOR THICK CARDS

1. Make a see through plastic pattern 2-3/8" by 3-1/4".
2. Center pattern over images and trace around thirteen pair of images and a single one for the Silly Goose.
3. Cut a piece each of vinyl wallpaper and poster board 14" by 21".
4. Paste them together. Put paper towels over them and dry overnight under weight. (This is the backing for the images.)
5. Use pattern to cut out a backing for each image.
6. Glue image on cardboard side of backing.
7. Dry under weight overnight.
8. (Thick cards have three layers: wallpaper back, poster board center and a wallpaper image top.)

DIRECTIONS FOR THIN CARDS

1. Follow directions for the thick cards, except omit the cardboard and paste two pieces of vinyl wallpaper back-to-back. Put paper towels over wallpaper and dry overnight under weight.

DIRECTIONS FOR CARD BOX

1. Cut a piece each of vinyl wallpaper and poster board 9" by 10".
2. Paste the wallpaper onto poster board. Dry under weight overnight.
3. Use pattern on page 105 and cut out box. Score on dotted lines and fold box. Glue side flap.
4. Glue an animal image on box and print name of game on front of box.

GENERAL INFORMATION

The game is played like Old Maid. Replace the Old Maid with Forgetful Fredie, Molly Monkey or Silly Goose. Twenty-seven thick cards fit into box. That provides three players with nine cards each.

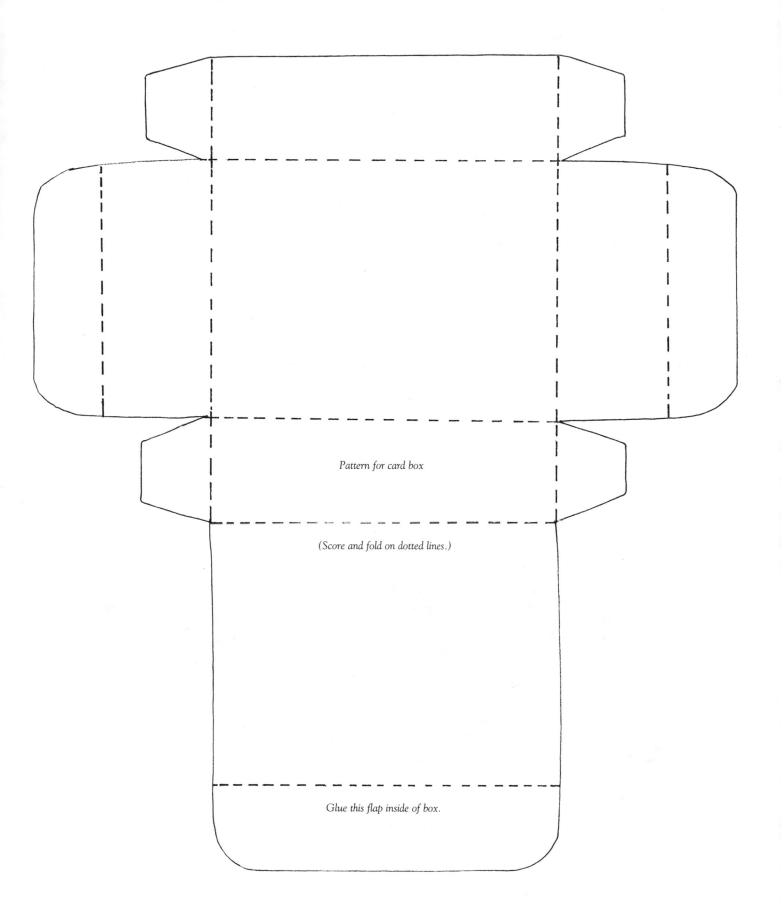

Pattern for card box

(Score and fold on dotted lines.)

Glue this flap inside of box.

Feather Headband   Lone Ranger Mask

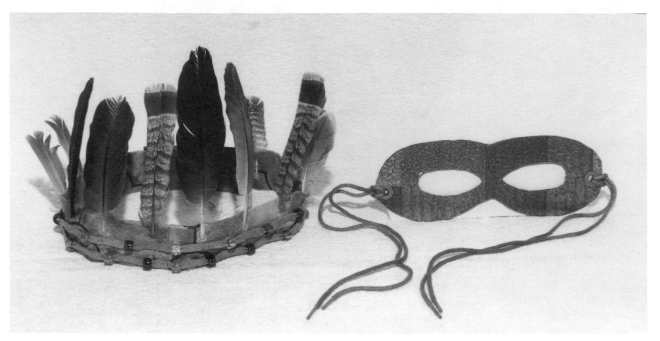

Illustration 207

MATERIALS FOR FEATHER BAND
Ruler, leather-like vinyl wallpaper, damp cloth, paper punch, scissors, two 21-1/2" by 1/4" leather strips, twelve small feathers, pony beads, glue, Velcro and brush.

MATERIALS FOR LONE RANGER MASK
Leather-like wallpaper, a matching 26" pair of shoe-strings, scissors, felt, paper punch, piece of leather to reinforce eyelets, glue and a damp cloth.

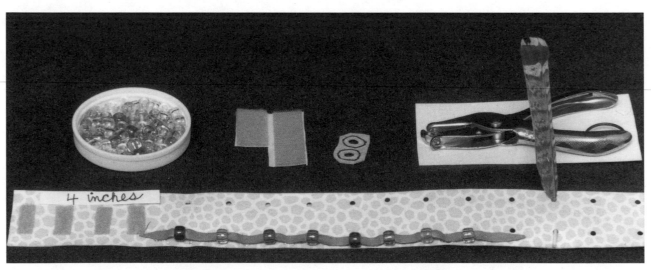

Illustration 208

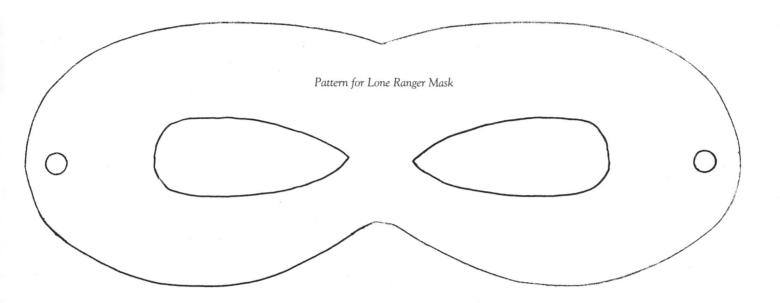

Pattern for Lone Ranger Mask

DIRECTIONS FOR FEATHER HEADBAND

1. Cut a strip of vinyl wallpaper 3" wide and 24-1/4" long. You can use an outdated wallpaper catalog, but you may have to piece the band. If necessary, you can also piece the leather strips.

2. Fold strip in half horizontally. Crease, then unfold and apply glue to bottom half. Fold over top half and press firmly with damp cloth.

3. Glue four, 1/4" pieces of Velcro on first end. (illustration 208)

4. Punch two holes above each other, 1/4" from top and bottom edges. (See illustration 208)

5. Keep on punching two holes (top and bottom) every 1-1/2" until you get to other end.

6. Glue other half of Velcro onto backside of other end. This will make headband adjustable.

7. Next, cut two strips of leather and thread beads 1-1/2" apart. Point end of leather so it will thread.

8. Glue a leather strip on bottom edge and one in the middle. Apply glue between the beads and press down with a toothpick. Dry well.

9. Then put the feathers in, with the tall ones in the front. Gently push the feathers through the top hole and out the bottom one. Continue to the end of headband.

DIRECTIONS FOR LONE RANGER MASK

1. Follow the pattern and cut two pieces of vinyl wallpaper 3" by 8". Glue back-to-back and dry overnight under weight.

2. Cut out mask. Enlarge eye openings if necessary so that child's vision will not be obstructed.

3. Use mask pattern and cut a felt backing.

4. Put a thin coat of glue on back of the mask and press on the felt.

5. Punch out eyelets in mask.

6. Next, make reinforcements for eyelet. Punch two holes in a piece of leather. Draw a circle around holes. (See illustration 208.)

7. Cut out and glue over holes in mask.

8. Attach strings to mask.

NOTE

Craft stores sell bright feathers. But you can save money by collecting your own. Besides, it's great fun. Look for them by lakes, bogs, and parks while vacationing. Make it a learning expedition. Try to identify the birds that shed the feathers.

Wind Fan

DIRECTIONS FOR WIND FAN

1. Cut a 12" piece from a 5/8" dowel.
2. Drill a hole 5/8" from the end of dowel with a 7/32" drill.
3. Sand off splinters.
4. Cut a 6" square piece of vinyl wallpaper.
5. Pencil a line kitty-cornered on the wrong side of square. Draw another line, making an X.
6. Cut a 1-1/2" circle from a piece of wallpaper and glue on the center of X.
7. Next, cut on lines to the edge of circle. (See illustration 210.)
8. Punch holes in every other corner, 1/2" from point. Now punch hole through center of circle for post.
9. Glue reinforcement rings around punch holes.
10. Glue strips of bright wallpaper across back of fan for color.
11. Cut a 1-1/4" piece of tubing.
12. Assemble fan as follows: Push post through hole in dowel. Place piece of tubing over post, then a washer and fan. Fold over fan corners. Add another washer and screw on post cap.

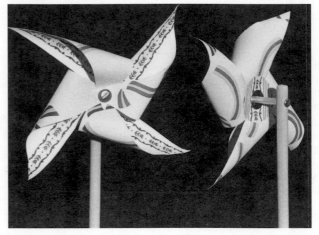

Illustration 209

MATERIALS FOR WIND FAN

Wallpaper, 7/32" drill, 5/32" O.D. plastic tubing, 2" posts, 7/32" washers, 7/16" drill, piece of leather, paper punch, 5/8" dowel, glue, scissors, ruler and damp cloth.

Illustration 210

Marching Drum

Illustration 211

MATERIALS FOR MARCHING DRUM

Glue, pony beads, two 1/8" bolts 3/4" long, a discarded chammy, belt, matching vinyl wallpaper, yardstick, a damp cloth, two 7" fruitcake tins 2-1/2" high, duck tape, ruler, 7/16" dowel, scissors, ruler and glue.

DIRECTIONS FOR MARCHING DRUM

1. Tape two fruitcake tins back-to-back with duct tape.
2. Next, cut a piece of wallpaper 3-15/16" by 23".
3. Mark wallpaper every 3-1/4" on top edge. Then, mark bottom edge every 3-1/4" between top marks. (See illustration 213.)
4. Glue wallpaper on tins.
5. Cut fourteen strips of chammy 4" by 1/4". Point ends and thread three beads on each one.
6. Dab glue on marks and between beds. Let glue set, then press on strip with toothpick. Finish gluing strips on.
7. Then, glue a 1/2" border strip on top and bottom over end of strip.
8. Drill two 1/8" holes in the middle side of each tin. (See illustration 212.)
9. Punch holes in belt and attach. Bolts are secured in each tin. Remove covers to attach nut to bolt.

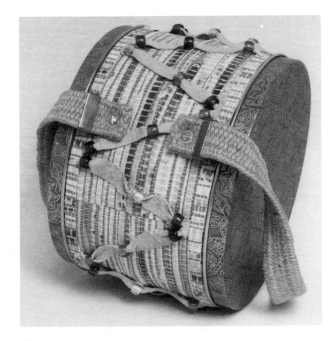

Illustration 212

DIRECTIONS FOR DRUMSTICKS

1. Cut two 11" pieces from dowel.
2. Cut two 1/2" by 6" strips from a chammy. Wind back and forth other end of dowel, gluing as you go.
3. Glue next strip crosswise over other strip.
4. Next, cut a strip 19" long and glue around end of dowel, stretching chammy as you go. Press with a damp cloth.

Illustration 213

Be sure to glue wallpaper to tins after marking it and before gluing on strips. Photo is shown only to expose a larger area.

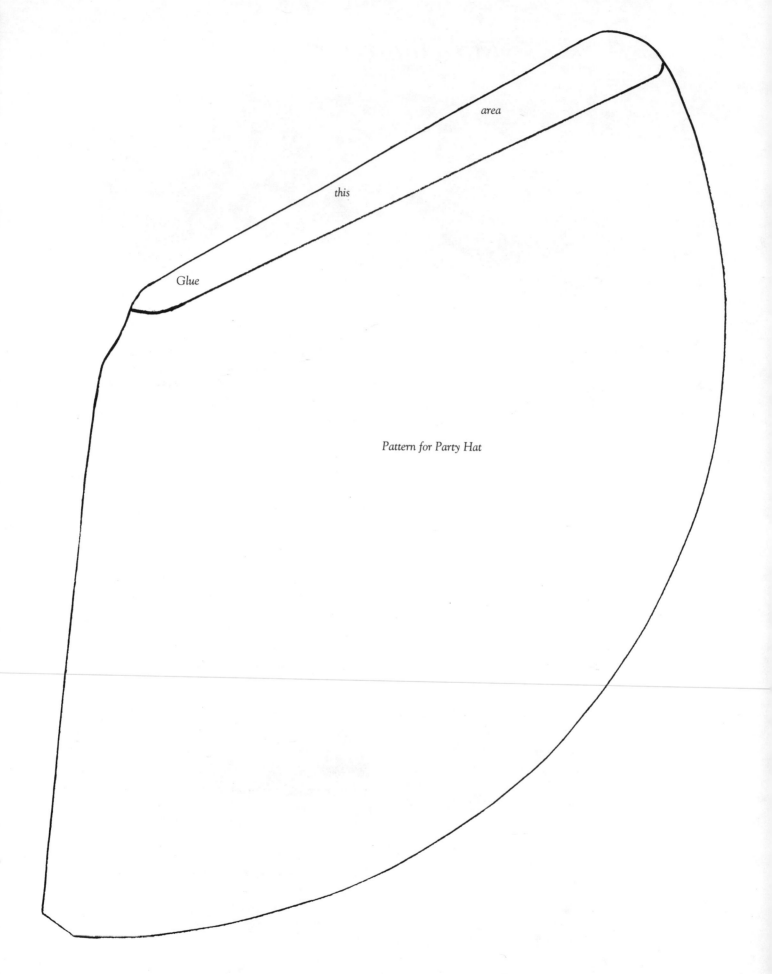

Glue

this

area

Pattern for Party Hat

Party Hats

Illustration 214

MATERIALS FOR PARTY HATS

Wallpaper, wallpaper image, round elastic cord, scissors, unthinned glue, small paper punch.

DIRECTIONS FOR PARTY HATS

1. Paste two pieces of wallpaper back-to-back. Dry under weight.
2. Cut out hat. Glue edge and roll into cone. Put paper clips on bottom and top until glue dries.
3. Glue a wallpaper image on hat.
4. Punch hole through sides of hat for chin cord.
5. Next cut off 20" of round elastic cord. Tie a triple knot on end of cord. Thread other end through hole from inside. Then thread cord through outside of hat and tie a triple knot on inside of hat.

DIRECTIONS FOR WALL PICTURE

1. Cut a piece of white wallpaper and foam core the size of frame.
2. Glue wallpaper on to foam core.
3. Then, glue image in the center of wallpaper. Dry overnight under weight.
4. Glue on moving eyes. Let dry.
5. Frame and attach hanger.

Child's Wall Picture

Illustration 215

MATERIALS FOR CHILD'S WALL PICTURE

Frame, vinyl wallpaper, foam core, wallpaper image, moving eyes, eye screws, glue, scissors and wire.

Bedtime Story Bookcase

Illustration 216

Illustration 217

MATERIALS FOR BEDTIME BOOKCASE

Assorted wallpaper, thick cardboard box, glue,
scissors, utility knife, ruler, scale model paint, masking
tape, size 5/0 brush for outlining, gluing brush and
damp cloth.

DIRECTIONS FOR BEDTIME BOOKCASE

1. Draw the two sides for bookcase. (See illustration
   218.) Then draw a line across back of box 10" high,
   connecting the two sides.
2. Cut out with utility knife.
3. Tape edges and seams with masking tape.
   (See illustration 216.)
4. Glue wallpaper on bookcase in a crazy quilt fashion, overlapping pieces on edges. Dry overnight.
5. Next, outline pieces with blue scale model paint.
   Dry overnight.
6. Last, glaze bookcase with thinned glue. Glaze top
   half first and dry overnight. Then tip over bookcase
   and do bottom half. Dry thoroughly before using.

NOTE

It is easier to outline and dry pieces before gluing the
inside corners in.

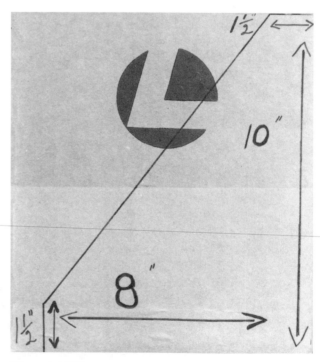

Illustration 218

Nursery Wall Picture

Illustration 219

Illustration 220

MATERIALS FOR NURSERY PICTURE

Frame, assorted wallpaper, moving eyes, white vinyl
wallpaper, brush for gluing, size 5/0 brush for outlining,
scissors, wallpaper animal image, foam core, damp
cloth, ruler and sky blue scale model paint.

DIRECTIONS FOR NURSERY PICTURE

1. Cut a piece of white wallpaper and foam core the
   size of frame.
2. Apply diluted glue to foam core and press on
   wallpaper, smoothing out with a damp cloth.
   Dry overnight under weight.
3. Glue animal image in center of wallpaper.
   Press out air with damp cloth. Dry overnight
   under light weight.
4. Glue on eyes. Dry overnight.
5. Frame. It needs no glass.

DIRECTIONS FOR CRAZY QUILT FRAME

1. Glue wallpaper pieces on front and back of frame
   in crazy quilt fashion. Dry overnight.
2. Outline pieces with scale model paint.
   Dry overnight.
3. Glaze frame with thinned glue. Dry thoroughly.

NOTE

You don't need a perfect frame for making nursery
pictures. Cover the corner cracks and dents with
masking tape. Snip edges of wallpaper in the corners
to avoid wrinkling. A group of three or more pictures
is an eye-catcher, especially when you have a crazy
quilt bedspread nearby. The difference between
wallpaper and cloth go unnoticed because the
designs and colors blend so well. And, of course,
the outlining ties it all together.

Take-With Toy Box

Illustration 221

Pattern for Toy Box Handle

MATERIALS FOR TAKE-WITH TOY BOX

A 12" square box (approximate), ruler, small brush for gluing, size 5/0 brush for outlining, masking tape, blue scale model paint, yardstick, scissors, assorted wallpaper, glue, utility knife and damp cloth.

DIRECTIONS FOR TAKE-WITH TOY BOX

1. Mark off a height of 12" around box. Then, trace handles on opposite sides, 1" from top of box.

2. Cut out box and handles with a utility knife.

3. Tape edge of handles and top of box with masking tape. (See illustration 216 for taping suggestion.)

4. Glue wallpaper on box in crazy quilt fashion, doing edges first.

5. When finished, dry overnight.

6. Next, outline pieces with blue scale model paint. Dry overnight.

7. Glaze entire toy box with thinned glue. (First do inside and top outside of box and dry thoroughly. Then, turn box upside down and do bottom.)

Teach your child to be responsible by letting him or her pack their own toys when you go on vacation or out visiting.

NOTE

If you think you will have a problem outlining inside bottom of box, outline the inside pieces before gluing them on box. (See illustration 75.) Let paint dry overnight before gluing on box because it may smear. Never outline pieces in black. Medium blue blends well with assorted wallpaper. You could also use wallpaper with images of stuffed animals and toys.

An appliance box is usually strong enough. Cut off excess height.

Turtles

Illustration 222

MATERIALS FOR TURTLES

Flat, round stone for body, long, flat stones for legs and head, scissors, toothpick, tiny moving eyes, black felt pen, glue, piece of black felt for tail and damp cloth.

DIRECTIONS FOR TURTLES

1. Wash and dry stones thoroughly.
2. Use body stone as a pattern and trace onto wallpaper. Cut out and glue onto stone, snipping edges to avoid wrinkles.
3. Glue on legs, head and tail.
4. Leave upside down overnight.
5. Dot glue on head for eyes. Let glue set, then press on eyes with aid of a toothpick. Dry two hours.
6. Glue a matching piece of wallpaper on bottom of turtle.
7. Next, draw oblong bars on shell with black felt pen. Do same on the bottom.

NOTE

The design of turtle shells differ somewhat. However most have oblong bars. Choose wallpaper in shades of green, orange, brown and yellow. Draw bars on shell with a black pen. Use undiluted glue.

Sea Monster

Illustration 223

DIRECTIONS FOR SEA MONSTER

1. Pick out a stone that could be made to look like a sea monster's face. Wash and dry stone.
2. Glue piece of felt to bottom of stone.
3. Next, cut out a bright colored, octopus-like design. Glue onto top of stone, with the arms hanging down the sides.
4. Glue on large moving eyes.

Baby's Bank

Illustration 224

Child's Bank

Illustration 225

NOTE

Above craft is made by tearing strips of wallpaper and gluing onto can, piece by piece. Refer to page 29 for directions and photos.

MATERIALS FOR BABY'S BANK

X-acto knife, soft wallpaper (not vinyl), Pringles potato chip can, moving eyes, glue, ruler and damp cloth.

DIRECTIONS FOR BABY'S BANK

1. Cut the top off from a Pringles potato chip can to 3-1/4".
2. Use X-acto knife to cut a slit 1/8" by 1" in the center of cover.
3. Glue strips of wallpaper around edge of slit, overlapping to back. Complete both sides of cover.
4. Now cover outside of can, overlap strips to inside.
5. Cut out a 2-3/4" circle and glue inside bottom. Press on with eraser end of pencil.
6. Cut a piece of wallpaper 9-1/2" by 3-1/16" and glue to inside of can.
7. Glue on image and eye. Let dry.
8. Use pliers to crimp edge outward so that cover snaps on.

MATERIALS FOR CHILD'S BANK

Ruler, child's wallpaper, scissors, glue, Calumet baking powder can, X-acto knife and damp cloth.

DIRECTIONS FOR CHILD'S BANK

1. Cut two pieces of wallpaper 3-5/8" by 8". Glue one on the inside, the other on the outside of can.
2. Cut a slit 1/8" by 1" in cover.
3. Cut out circle of wallpaper for top of cover. *Do not cut hole yet.* Glue onto cover and dry overnight.
4. Put cover on a board, backside up and cut on dotted lines where indicated. Push tabs through slit and glue down on back.
5. Cut a strip of wallpaper 7/16" by 1". Crease in center lengthwise.
6. Glue one on each side of hole. (See illustration 225.) Then glue a piece of wallpaper across ends.
7. Last, cut out slit on wallpaper for back of cover and glue on.

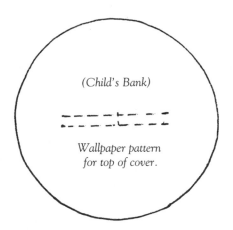

(Child's Bank)

*Wallpaper pattern
for top of cover.*

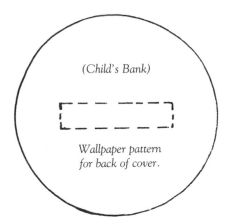

(Child's Bank)

*Wallpaper pattern
for back of cover.*

NOTE
Glue paper on cover and dry *before* you cut on dotted lines.

NOTE
Cut hole *before* gluing onto back of cover.

Illustration 226

Pen and Crayon Box

MATERIALS FOR PEN AND CRAYON BOX
Wallpaper, utility knife, marker, 1/2 gallon milk carton, glue, ruler, Congoleum, scissors, moving eyes, wallpaper image and cardboard.

DIRECTIONS FOR PEN AND CRAYON BOX
1. Cut carton down to 3-3/8".
2. Glue a 4-1/2" square of wallpaper on bottom of carton. Overlap sides.
3. Cut a 3-7/8" square for inside.
4. Next, glue a strip 3-1/2" by 16" on outside of box. Overlap to inside.
5. Glue a piece 3-1/4" by 15" inside.
6. Cut wallpaper for divider from pattern on page 118. (Cover front and back.)
7. Cut out false bottom. Score and crease on dotted lines.
8. Glue wallpaper on outside. Fold and glue end tab inside. Glue to bottom of divider. (See illustration 228.) Glue inside of box.
9. Glue image on wrong side of Congoleum. Dry under weight. Cut out.
10. Glue image on box, then eye.

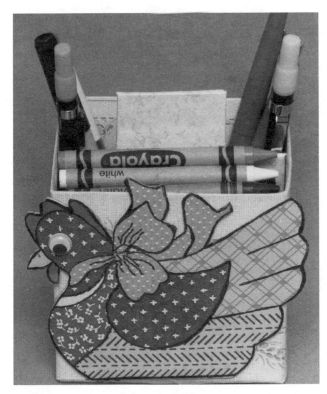

Illustration 227

Divider

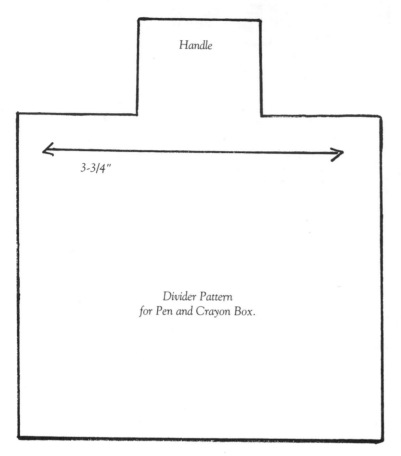

Handle

3-3/4"

*Divider Pattern
for Pen and Crayon Box.*

Illustration 228

Cardboard from the back of a wide tablet will work fine, but poster board is too thin to hold up under the weight of the crayons.

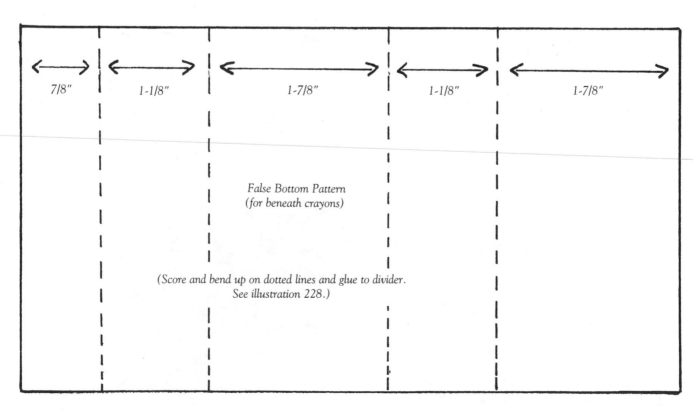

7/8" | 1-1/8" | 1-7/8" | 1-1/8" | 1-7/8"

*False Bottom Pattern
(for beneath crayons)*

*(Score and bend up on dotted lines and glue to divider.
See illustration 228.)*

Spam Color Box

Illustration 229

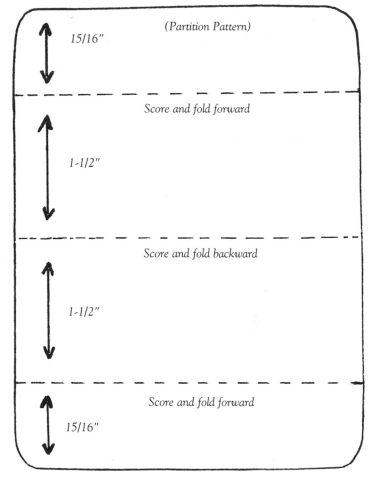

(Partition Pattern)

15/16"

Score and fold forward

1-1/2"

Score and fold backward

1-1/2"

Score and fold forward

15/16"

Materials for Spam Color Box

Damp cloth, scissors, Spam can, wallpaper, thin cardboard, brush, ruler and glue.

Directions for Spam Color Box

1. Wash can thoroughly with brush and soapsuds.
2. Then, use pliers to press down sharp edges.
3. Cut two pieces of wallpaper 1-7/8" by 11-1/2". Glue one piece inside and the other piece on the outside of can. Press out air bubbles with a damp cloth.
4. Cover bottom inside and outside with wallpaper.

Note

Score and bend the partition cardboard *before* you cover it with wallpaper.

The Spam can makes an ideal color box, especially for the short color crayons.

Directions for Partition

1. Cut out partition from a piece of thin cardboard.
2. Score and bend on dotted lines.
3. Glue wallpaper on cardboard and dry under weight.
4. Glue partition together before inserting in can.

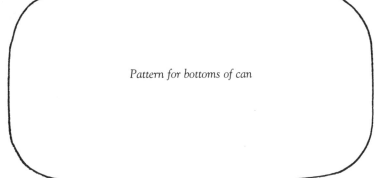

Pattern for bottoms of can

3-D Crayon Box

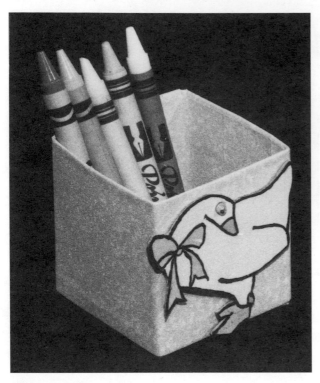

Illustration 230

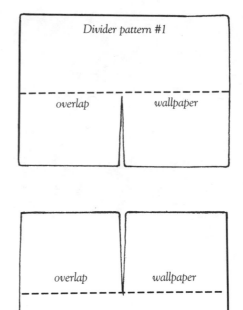

Divider pattern #1

overlap   wallpaper

overlap   wallpaper

Divider pattern #2

Small children will enjoy putting away the crayons in this fascinating box.

MATERIALS FOR 3-D CRAYON BOX

Ruler, glue, wallpaper, small moving eye, scissors, brush, piece of Congoleum, image of a nursery rhyme character, 8 oz. milk carton and a damp cloth.

DIRECTIONS FOR 3-D CRAYON BOX

1. Wash carton, then cut to height of 2-1/4".
2. Cut a piece of wallpaper 2-3/4" by 9-1/2" for outside of carton. (This allows for overlap on top and bottom.)
3. Next cut a piece of wallpaper 2-1/4" by 9-1/2" for the inside.
4. Glue a 2-1/4" square on inside and outside bottom of carton.
5. Glue image on back side of Congoleum . Dry under weight.
6. Cut out and glue on box. (Leave flat until dry.) Glue on eye.

DIRECTIONS FOR DIVIDER

1. Cut two pieces of wallpaper 2-3/8" by 3-1/2" and glue on cardboard. Overlap on dotted line.
2. Cut a 3/4" slot in center of each cardboard. (See illustration 231.)
3. Put cardboard #1 in the slot of #2 and slide into box.

Box Divider

Illustration 231

Paper Dolls

Illustration 232

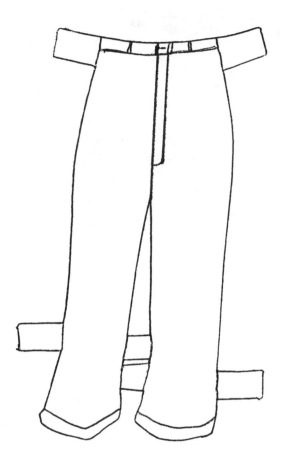

NOTE

Always use miniature designed wallpaper for doll clothes. Put a strip of masking tape on back of tabs, extending beyond bend. (The tape keeps tab from wearing.)

MATERIALS FOR PAPER DOLL

Scissors, utility knife, plain and miniature designed wallpaper, dark and light cardboard for dolls, an extra fine point marker, damp cloth, ruler and glue.

DIRECTIONS FOR PAPER DOLLS

1. Trace dolls onto thin cardboard and cut out. (patterns on page 121)
2. Draw in hair and faces.
3. Then, color eyes, hair, cheeks, lips and shoes.
4. Cut out pattern (A) and (B) for doll's platform. (Optional: Cover back and front with wallpaper. Dry overnight under weight.)
5. Next, cut out notches and slots for feet. Put doll's feet through slots. If legs are spindly, reinforce them by gluing narrow strips of cardboard behind legs.
6. Bend (B) in half and attach (A). (See sketch on page 123.)
7. Now, make clothes for the dolls out of miniature designed wallpaper. Choosing the right texture is important. Example: The straw hat and knit knee-highs look authentic because of the wallpaper texture. Get a sample catalog and have fun making new outfits.

(B)

Cut out on dotted lines

Stand-up platform for doll (A)

NOTE
Doll patterns are on page 121.

Back view of
platform

123

Refrigerator Magnets

MATERIALS FOR MAGNETS
Ball point marker for outlining, glue, toothpick, Congoleum, moving eyes, damp cloth, scissors, wallpaper images, magnetic tape, scale model paint, size 5/0 brush, pink felt and brush for gluing.

DIRECTIONS FOR MAGNETS
1. Glue images onto wrong side of Congoleum. (See illustration 234.) Dry overnight under weight.
2. Outline images with a fine ball point marker. Let dry.
3. Then, cut out images and paint the edge of Congoleum. (This seals the wallpaper so it won't separate from the Congoleum.) Dry overnight.
4. Cut off 1" of magnetic tape and shape in an oval. Apply a small amount of glue on the back of each image. Place magnet over glue. Dry overnight under weight.
5. Next, glue pieces of pink felt on ears and nose of image. Use any other decor you choose, depending on type of image. Last, glue on moving eyes.

NOTE
Use a toothpick to guide the felt and eyes when gluing them on.

Illustration 233

Illustration 234

Gift Box/Gift Tag Gift Wrap/Gift Card

Illustration 235

Illustration 236

MATERIALS FOR GIFT WRAP

Scissors, children's wallpaper, ribbon, box, yardstick and transparent tape.

DIRECTIONS FOR GIFT WRAP

1. Wrap box with children's wallpaper as you would with any gift wrapping paper. Tape ends.
2. Tie with matching ribbon.

DIRECTIONS FOR CHILD'S GIFT CARD

1. Cut out an image from the same wallpaper used to wrap the gift.
2. Cover a piece of thin cardboard with 3" by 5" plain wallpaper.
3. Dry overnight under weight.
4. Score and fold in half lengthwise.
5. Glue image on front of card. If needed, adjust cardboard measurement to fit your image. Write greetings inside.

NOTE

The above wallpaper pattern is used for several different projects. Two examples are the valentines (See illustration 246.) and the refrigerator magnets. (See illustration 233.)

MATERIALS FOR GIFT BOX

Children's wallpaper, scissors, ruler, ribbon, wallpaper paste, box, damp cloth and cardboard for tag.

DIRECTIONS FOR GIFT BOX

1. Place box on the wrong side of wallpaper and outline bottom.
2. Then measure the height of your box, add 1/2" for overlap to inside. Use this figure to draw a line beyond the box outline. (See illustration 165.)
3. Draw a line across end and snip corners.
4. Apply paste to wallpaper. Place box on outline, fold up ends and overlap to inside.
5. Paste down sides, then do cover likewise.

DIRECTIONS FOR GIFT TAG

1. Pick an image that matches box.
2. Glue image onto cardboard. Let dry under weight.
3. Punch hole in tag for ribbon.

Stand-Up Greeting Cards

Illustration 237

MATERIALS FOR CHILD'S CARDS

Glue, scissors, wallpaper images, moving eyes, marker for outlining, brush, damp cloth and thin cardboard or poster board.

DIRECTIONS FOR CHILD'S CARDS

1. Cut out wallpaper image.
2. Cut a piece of cardboard that is double the size of the image.
3. Score center of cardboard, then fold.
4. Glue image on fold of cardboard and dry overnight under weight.
5. Glue on moving eyes. Dry overnight.
6. Write greetings inside.

OPTIONAL

Learn calligraphy to add a professional edge to your cards. Calligraphy is taught in many community education classes.

NOTE

Place either the top or side of image on fold of cardboard. (It depends on the form of image.)

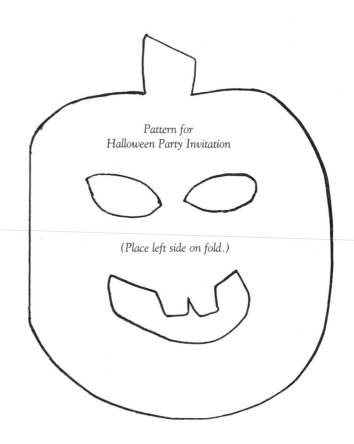

Pattern for Halloween Party Invitation

(Place left side on fold.)

Child's Deluxe Card

llustatration 238

IIllustration 239

DIRECTIONS FOR DELUXE CARDS

1. Glue wallpaper image on fold of poster board. Dry under weight.
2. Cut out. Add any decoration you wish. (Socks, ribbon, moving eyes, string for tail, felt for ears and nose and cotton for bunny tail are all possible decorations.)
3. Write greetings inside.

DIRECTIONS FOR HALLOWEEN PARTY INVITATIONS

1. Cut out jack-o'-lantern from any shade of orange or rust colored wallpaper.
2. Next, glue yellow wallpaper behind eyes and mouth.
3. Glue in white teeth and a green stem.
4. Glue jack-o'-lantern on fold of thin cardboard. Place left side on fold so it opens from the right. Dry overnight under weight.
5. Cut out, then write invitation inside.

NOTE

Envelope pattern is on page 128.

NOTE

Moving eyes, socks and ribbon were added to complement above card.

Halloween Party Invitation

Illustration 240

127

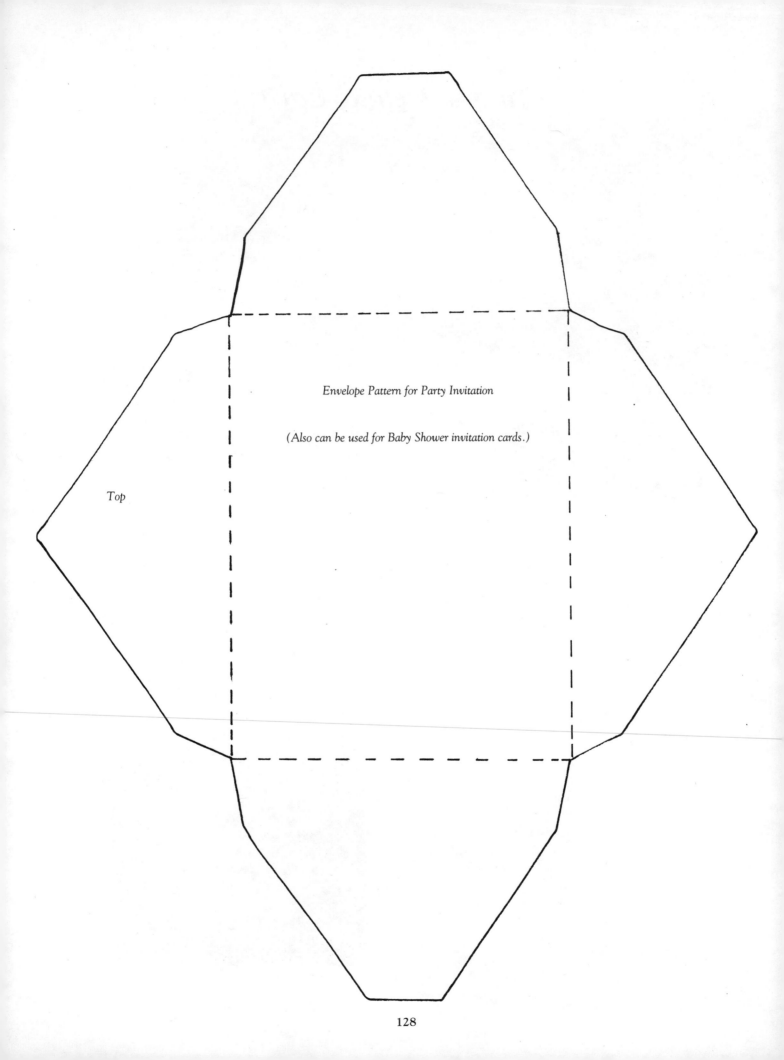

Envelope Pattern for Party Invitation

(Also can be used for Baby Shower invitation cards.)

Top

Shower Invitation

Illustration 241

Illustration 242

MATERIALS FOR SHOWER INVITATION
Wallpaper image, scissors, ruler, ribbon, glue, poster board, brush and damp cloth.

DIRECTIONS FOR SHOWER INVITATIONS
1. Use a 2-3/4" by 3-3/4" plastic pattern to draw around wallpaper image.
2. Glue image onto front of folded poster board.
3. Leave folded and dry overnight under weight. Outline image.
4. Glue on decorations. Dry overnight. Print invitation inside.

Pattern for Baby Shower Card (cut from poster board.)

Score and fold

(Glue image here.)

Single Valentines

Illustration 243

MATERIALS FOR SINGLE VALENTINES

Wallpaper images, scissors, ruler, thin cardboard, glue, red wallpaper for hearts, permanent marker, brush and damp cloth.

DIRECTIONS FOR SINGLE VALENTINES

1. Cut out wallpaper images.
2. Next, glue them onto thin cardboard. Wipe off surface glue with a damp cloth. Dry under weight.
3. Glue small hearts on cardboard and dry under weight.
4. Then, outline the images with a black marker. Cut out the images and small hearts.
5. Cut a V or slit in the mouth of image to hold a small heart.
6. Glue heart under V or in mouth slit.
7. Write a love message on heart.

NOTE

The small heart pattern is on page 132.

Illustration 244

Double Valentines

Illustration 245

Illustration 246

MATERIALS FOR DOUBLE VALENTINES
Permanent marker, shades of red or pink vinyl wallpaper, ruler, scissors, wallpaper images, thin cardboard, utility knife, brush, glue and damp cloth.

DIRECTIONS FOR DOUBLE VALENTINES
1. Cut out hearts from vinyl wallpaper.
2. Glue large hearts onto fold of thin cardboard.
3. Glue small hearts onto single thickness of cardboard.
4. Wipe off surface glue with damp cloth and dry under weight.
5. Outline and cut out images.
6. Cut V or slit in mouths to hold small heart.
7. Glue images in center of large heart. Glue small hearts in mouth. Wipe off surface glue, Dry overnight under weight.
8. Write a love message on small heart, then, write a verse inside valentine.

NOTE
Adust size of heart to fit your wallpaper images. Heart patterns are on page 132.

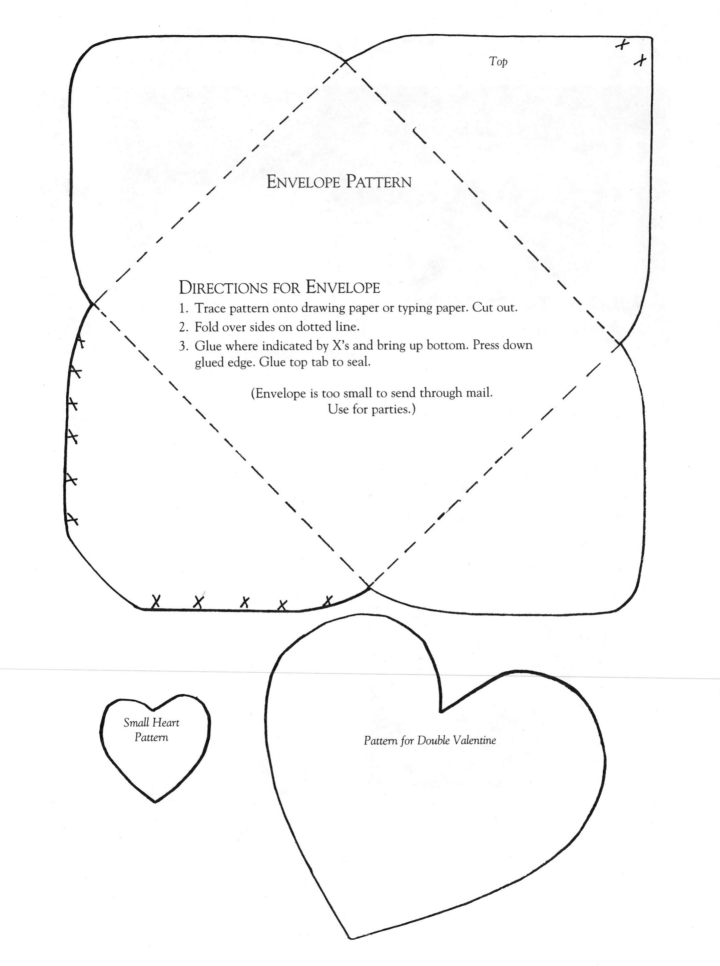

Top

ENVELOPE PATTERN

DIRECTIONS FOR ENVELOPE

1. Trace pattern onto drawing paper or typing paper. Cut out.
2. Fold over sides on dotted line.
3. Glue where indicated by X's and bring up bottom. Press down glued edge. Glue top tab to seal.

(Envelope is too small to send through mail. Use for parties.)

Small Heart Pattern

Pattern for Double Valentine

Sunday School Craft

Nut Basket/Place Card

Illustration 247

Illustration 248

MATERIALS FOR NUT BASKET SET

Ruler, miniature designed wallpaper, wallpaper paste, permanent marker for name card, scissors, 2-1/2" bake-cups, cardboard, glue, brush, damp cloth and stapler.

DIRECTIONS FOR NUT BASKET

1. Paste two pieces of vinyl wallpaper back-to-back. Dry overnight under weight.
2. Trace circle patterns and handles 1/2" by 6-1/2". (See illustration 249.)
3. Center bottom pattern on circle and trace. Cut out circle, and cut on dotted lines where indicated.
4. Crease sides and end tabs.
5. Bend tabs around corner, then end of handle. Bring end of basket up and staple. (See illustration 248.)
6. Repeat with other end. Insert bake cup.
7. Complete rest of baskets.

Making nut baskets and place cards for the Mother and Daughter Banquet is a good project for a junior high Sunday school class.

DIRECTIONS FOR PLACE CARDS

1. Cut out place card from poster board. Score and fold in half.
2. Bend trim in half lengthwise, don't crease middle. Cut edge with pinking shears. Then, cut out center. (See illustration 249.)

NOTE

If you don't have a pinking shears, just use a scissors.

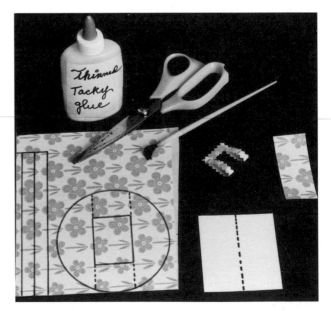

Illustration 249

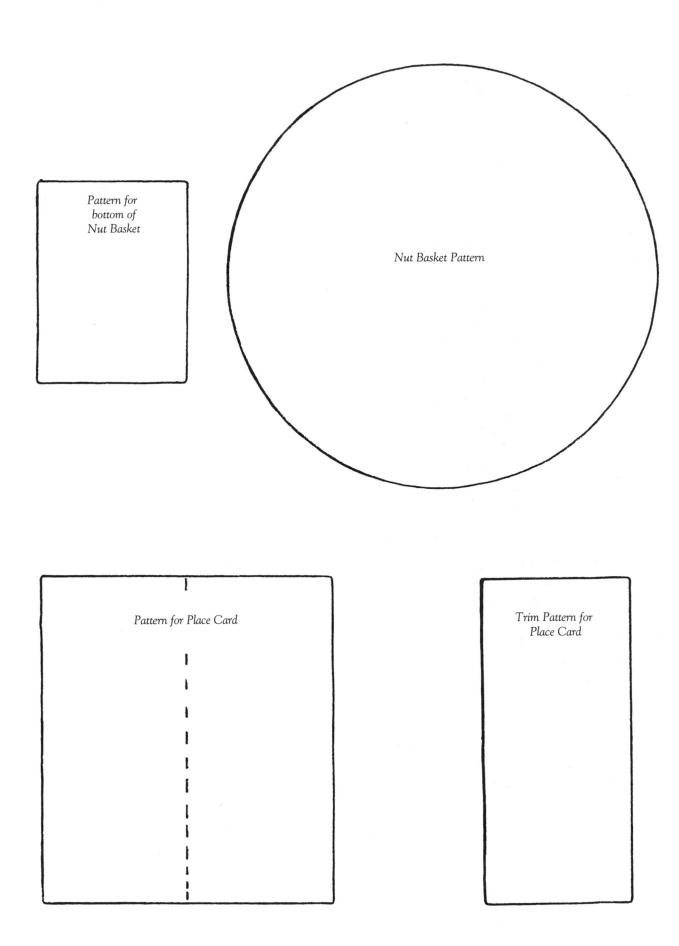

Pattern for
bottom of
Nut Basket

Nut Basket Pattern

Pattern for Place Card

Trim Pattern for
Place Card

Oatmeal Box Basket

Illustration 250

Easter and spring are symbolic. In designing your centerpiece, try to capture the sudden awakening which distinguishes the Easter season.

DIRECTIONS FOR ARRANGING OATMEAL BOX BASKET

1. Glue a small piece of Styrofoam 1" thick in center of box.
2. Make a hole in center of Styrofoam to anchor cross.
3. Put tall flowers or vine behind and to the sides of cross.
4. Add artificial grass and eggs.
5. Poke short stems of flowers between eggs.

NOTE

Mix a dab of main color with acrylic white to obtain a lighter more delicate shade.

MATERIALS FOR OATMEAL BOX BASKET

Large oatmeal box, scissors, ruler, artificial grass, Styrofoam, glitter, glue, wallpaper paste, brush, acrylic paint, small wooden cross, Styrofoam eggs, rayon flowers and damp cloth.

DIRECTIONS FOR OATMEAL BOX BASKET

1. Follow directions for Shoe Box Basket in cutting out your oatmeal basket. (Follow steps 1 and 2.)
2. Place oatmeal box on cardboard and trace outline. Cut out and glue on bottom. (This will create a reinforcement for bottom.)
3. Cover cardboard with wallpaper and glue on bottom of box.
4. Cut a piece of wallpaper 3-1/8" by 18" and paste around box.
5. Cut wallpaper in center of triangles. (See illustration 252.)
6. Apply glue to tab and glue down one side. Trim off wallpaper even with tab and do other side.
7. Finish box. Then, paste a strip of wallpaper below tabs, to cover box that shows above grass.

NOTE

Use wallpaper paste to paste wallpaper to box, but use glue for tabs.

MATERIALS FOR MAKING EGGS

Styrofoam eggs, diamond glitter, acrylic paint (or any leftover water based paint), brush, headless thin nail, a bowl to catch excess glitter and damp cloth.

DIRECTIONS FOR PAINTING EGGS

1. Stick a thin nail into a Styrofoam egg. (Use as handle when you paint egg.) Paint several eggs.
2. Sprinkle wet eggs with diamond glitter and lay on brown paper.
3. Allow one hour to dry. Turn over egg so bottom dries before you put it in basket.

Shoe Box Basket

MATERIALS FOR SHOE BOX BASKET

Lady's shoe box, floral wallpaper, artificial grass, Styrofoam, glitter, glue, wallpaper paste, ruler, acrylic paint, scissors, Styrofoam eggs, damp cloth and brushes.

DIRECTIONS FOR SHOE BOX BASKET

1. Cut box to 3" high.
2. Draw a line around box 1" down from top. Then, mark off 1" intervals on line. Draw triangles and cut out. (See illustration 252.)
3. Put box on wrong side of wallpaper and outline.
4. Now draw a line 3-1/4" beyond outline of box.
5. Apply paste to wallpaper. Place box on outline.
6. Cut out corners. (See illustration 165.) Bring up ends. Now bring up sides and press paper to box.
7. Snip paper in center of triangle. (See illustration 252.)
8. Glue one side of tab down, trim off excess wallpaper and glue down other side of tabs. Continue around box.
9. Paste strip of wallpaper below tabs to cover what will show above grass.

Illustration 251

DIRECTIONS FOR ARRANGING SHOE BOX

1. Cut a 2" thick piece of Styrofoam 3" by 6". Glue it in the center of box. Dry overnight.
2. Put in artificial grass.
3. Push flowers into Styrofoam.
4. Arrange eggs. Add tiny flowers between eggs.

Illustration 252

Dove Centerpiece

Illustration 253

MATERIALS FOR DOVE CENTERPIECE

Small oatmeal box, flowered wallpaper, small dove, scissors, glue, small size chenille bumps for pussy willows, floral tape, floral moss, Styrofoam pigeon eggs, damp cloth, lilac twigs, sandpaper and utility knife.

DIRECTIONS FOR BASKET

1. Cut a small oatmeal box down to 2" high.
2. Cut a strip of wallpaper 2-1/4" by 13-1/4".
3. Glue around box, overlapping to inside.
4. Then, cut a 1/2" strip and glue below overlap, inside edge of box.
5. Wipe off glue with damp cloth.

DIRECTIONS FOR PUSSY WILLOWS

1. Trim five twigs varying from 3" to 6".
2. Using floral tape, start at top of twig and wind pussy willows to stem. Be sure to pull the tape tight. (See illustration 67.)
3. Leave twig bare at bottom so it will push into Styrofoam easily.
4. If you wish to make pussy willows appear thicker, pull chenille bumps out from stem.

DIRECTIONS FOR ARRANGING BASKET

1. Glue a 2" square of Styrofoam on side of basket. (This will be the base for pussy willows.)
2. Spread floral moss in bottom of basket and over Styrofoam.
3. Stick pussy willow stems into Styrofoam. (Put the tallest one in the center.)
4. Add eggs in front and bird between the eggs and pussy willows.

NOTE

If eggs are too large, whittle them down with an X-acto knife and sandpaper smooth.

Illustration 254

Name Tags

Egg Cup

Illustration 255

Illustration 256

MATERIALS FOR NAME TAGS

Wallpaper flowers, typing paper, glue, scissors, ruler, marking pen and pins.

DIRECTIONS FOR NAME TAGS

1. Mark off tags 1-1/2" by 4" on a piece of typing paper. (See illustration 254).

2. Then, cut out flower from miniature flowered wallpaper.

3. Glue on a piece of green thread for stem and some green leaves.

4. Write name in with a marker and pin name tag on person.

MATERIALS FOR EGG CUP

Glue, ruler, utility knife, Styrofoam cups, 2" baking cups, damp cloth, scissors and flowered wallpaper.

DIRECTIONS FOR EGG CUP

1. Trace pattern on the wrong side of flowered wallpaper.

2. Cut a Styrofoam cup down to 1-5/8" high.

3. Now glue wallpaper on cup. Snip overlap to edge of cup in 1/2" intervals. Then, fold down every other tab. Go back and glue down remaining tabs.

4. Insert matching baking cups.

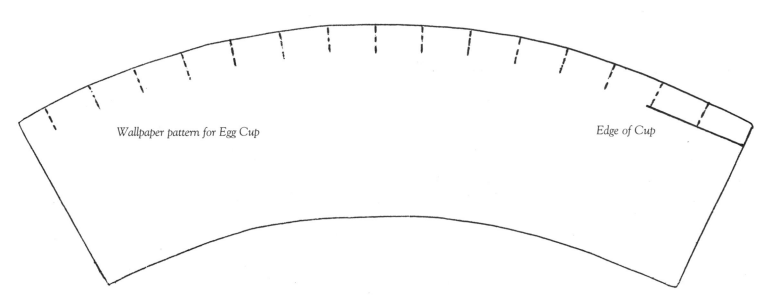

Wallpaper pattern for Egg Cup

Edge of Cup

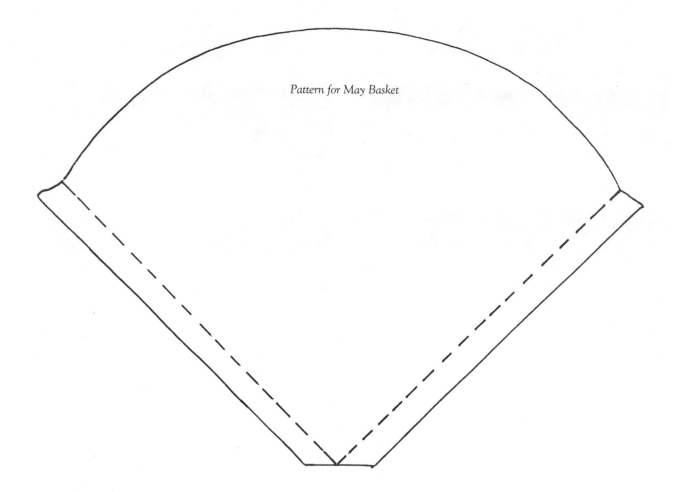

Pattern for May Basket

Handle Pattern   ⭘   Punch a small hole in center of handle for string.

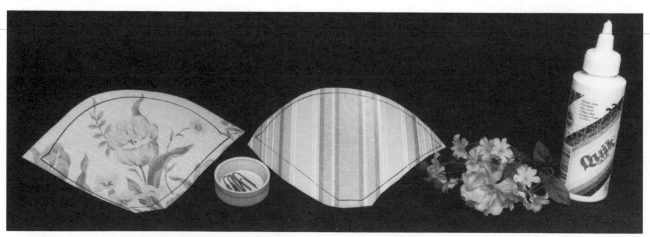

Illustration 257

May Basket Mobile

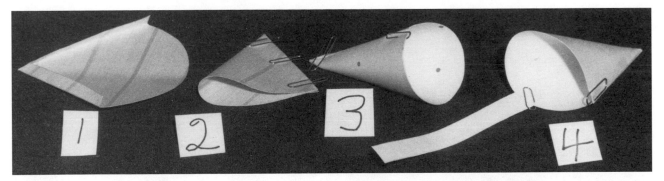

Illustration 258

MATERIALS FOR MAY BASKETS

Wallpaper, rayon flowers, glue, wallpaper paste, brush, scissors and paper clips.

DIRECTIONS FOR MAY BASKET

1. Paste two sheets of wallpaper back-to-back.
2. Dry overnight under weight.
3. Trace basket pattern and handle onto double wallpaper and cut out.
4. Fold edges on dotted lines. (See #1 in illustration 258.)
5. Apply glue to folded edge. Now, bring over other edge and clip together until glue is dry. (See #2 in illustration 258.)
6. Then, open basket and clip top and bottom to straighten. (See #3 in illustration 258.)
7. Glue end of handle and clip inside of basket. (See #4 in illustration 258.)

MATERIALS FOR MOBILE

White spray paint, two slats 14" long, string, five small screw eyes, yardstick and 1/2" screw hook.

DIRECTIONS FOR MOBILE

1. Spray slats white and dry well.
2. Pilot hole in the center of the slats and attach screw hook.
3. Attach screw eye under each end and under middle of slat.
4. Tie a triple knot in string and thread through hole in handle. Attach other end to screw eye. Vary lengths of string.
5. Arrange flowers in basket.
6. Then, make four more baskets.

Illustration 259

141

Disciple Finger Puppets

Illustration 260

Illustration 261

MATERIALS FOR DISCIPLE PUPPETS

Cardboard core from aluminum foil, paper towels to round head, ruler, black permanent marker, cardboard, flesh-colored wallpaper, scissors, cloth remnants, glue, red wallpaper for mouth, utility knife and fantasy fur or human hair.

DIRECTIONS FOR DISCIPLE PUPPETS

1. Cut a piece of core 2-1/2" long.
2. Stuff top 1/3 of core with paper towels to make head round.
3. Glue a piece of flesh-colored wallpaper 2-1/2" by 6" around core.
4. Draw in eyes and eyebrows with a permanent black marker.
5. Nose: Glue flesh-colored wallpaper onto cardboard. Dry overnight under weight. Then, fold cardboard and cut off corner for nose. (See illustration 261.) Glue onto face.
6. Cut out mouth and glue a piece of red wallpaper under cut-out.
7. Dab in white teeth with toothpick. Then, outline lips in red.
8. Glue on beard.
9. Cut a 6-3/4" circle of cloth.
10. Fold under edge 1" and glue on edge of forehead. Next, turn under side and glue down. (See illustration 262). Do other side and tie band around head.
11. Cut a 12-1/2" circle of cloth to cover hand.

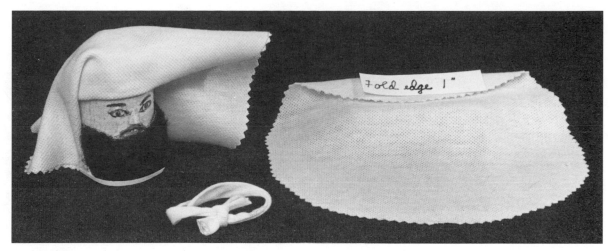

Illustration 262

Lesson Aid

MATERIALS FOR LESSON AID

A bright piece of wallpaper, brush, ruler, scissors, glue, poster board and a picture from a previous lesson that identifies with current lesson.

DIRECTIONS FOR LESSON AID

1. Place picture on wrong side of wallpaper and outline.
2. Now draw a line 1-1/2" beyond outline. Glue picture on wallpaper.
3. Next, glue them onto cardboard. Cut out, leaving border.
4. Stand-up brace: Cut a piece of cardboard 2" wide and 3/5 of height of cardboard. Bend 1" from end and glue creased end onto cardboard.
5. Dry overnight under weight.
6. Display in front of class for a visual aid to the lesson.

Illustration 263

Illustration 264

Sunshine Tree

MATERIALS FOR SUNSHINE TREE

Glue, container about 2" across and 2-1/2" tall, plaster of Paris, cardboard, scissors, brush, yellow wallpaper, lilac branch, child's photo, ribbon and damp cloth.

DIRECTIONS FOR SUNSHINE TREE

1. Trim leaves off of branch
2. Glue yellow wallpaper onto container.
3. Next, mix plaster of Paris according to directions and pour into container.
4. Push branch into plaster before it hardens.
5. Draw a facsimile of pattern on yellow wallpaper and cardboard.
6. Now glue them together.
7. Glue on photo. Put a paper towel over photo and dry under weight overnight.
8. Punch two small holes in top of frame.
9. Put ribbon through holes, tie a knot and curl ends. Hang on tree.

NOTE

The Sunshine Tree provides a sense of worth and acceptance. Ask your class if they have a small photo, otherwise you can take some snapshots.

Illustration 266

Grade Signs

Illustration 265

MATERIALS FOR GRADE SIGN

Wallpaper, 12" square of foam core, ruler, utility knife, brush, pinking shears, Bible story picture, glue and damp cloth.

DIRECTIONS FOR GRADE SIGN

1. Glue Bible story picture onto a bright piece of wallpaper that is 1" larger than picture.
2. Glue both onto a piece of foam core. Leave a space below picture for grade numbers. (See illustration 265.)
3. Cut out grade numbers and letters from matching wallpaper. Glue below picture.
4. Punch two holes in top edge of foam core and tie ribbon.
5. Hang sign on the outside of the Sunday school classroom.

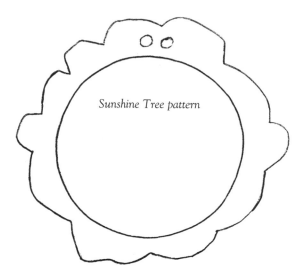

Sunshine Tree pattern

Pocket Bookmark

Illustration 267

MATERIALS FOR POCKET BOOKMARK

Vinyl wallpaper, scissors, wallpaper paste, cardboard, brush, small wallpaper flower and damp cloth.

DIRECTIONS FOR POCKET BOOKMARK

1. Paste two pieces of vinyl wallpaper back-to-back. Dry overnight under weight.
2. Fold wallpaper in half. Place pattern on fold and trace. Cut out.
3. Cut out pocket pattern. Glue a trim around edge and small flower in the center.
4. Glue pocket inside of bookmark.

NOTE

The teacher writes in verses as child learns them. (both sides)

(Patterns are on page 146.)

Illustration 268

Noah's Ark Stencils

Illustration 269

Pocket Bookmark Pattern

Place arrow side on fold of wallpaper

Pattern for cardboard insert

MATERIALS FOR NOAH'S ARK STENCILS

Wallpaper animal images, scissors, X-acto knife and poster board.

DIRECTIONS FOR NOAH'S ARK STENCILS

1. Cut out an 8" square of colored poster board. (Choose a color that matches the color of the animals.)
2. Trace image onto cardboard.
3. Put square on board and cut out traced animal with X-acto knife.
4. Save the center piece for tracing around, also.

NOTE

Stencils always fascinate children of kindergarten age. Choose simple wallpaper animal profiles.

Pocket Pattern

Apply glue to sides and bottom edge only. (use a toothpick.)

Easter Bookmark

Illustration 270

Crossbar
for
Bookmark

Easter
Bookmar
Pattern

MATERIALS FOR EASTER BOOKMARK
Paper punch, scissors, brush, ruler, wood-like wallpaper, yarn, cardboard and damp cloth.

DIRECTIONS FOR EASTER BOOKMARK
1. Trace patterns on wrong side of wood grained wallpaper. Cut out.
2. Next, glue them onto cardboard. Dry under weight overnight.
3. Cut them out and glue the short one across the top of other one to form a cross.
4. Punch a hole near top and tie a tassel. (See illustration 270.)

Rock Paperweight

Illustration 271

OPTIONAL
Glue a piece of magnetic tape on the edge of wallpaper. Let dry, then place a butterfly over magnet. (Directions for small butterfly is on page 13.)

DIRECTIONS FOR ROCK PAPERWEIGHT
1. Find an interesting rock that is flat on at least two sides. Scrub it clean.
2. Then, choose a subtle designed wallpaper with a smooth surface.
3. Type a Bible verse onto wallpaper.
4. Next, cut around the verse with a pinking shears. Glue verse onto rock.

Apple Tree Attendance Chart

Illustration 272

MATERIALS FOR TREE CHART

Brownish wallpaper for trunk, green wallpaper for rest of tree, red and yellow wallpaper for apples, poster board, gluing brush, size 5/0 brush, glue, scissors, scale model paint, ruler and damp cloth.

DIRECTIONS FOR TREE CHART

1. Cut out trees and trunks. (each poster board holds nine trees.) If more poster board is needed, tape seven more inches onto side.

2. Arrange and glue trees on poster board. Place paper towels over trees and dry under weight.

3. Cut out apples. Then, paint the stems and leaves. Dry well. (Store extra ones in envelope.)

4. Type a nameplate for each student and tape under their tree.

5. Attach chart to wall.

6. Tape an apple onto child's tree each Sunday he or she is present.

NOTE

Cut off a piece of tape 3/8" and form into a roll with sticky side out. Flatten and tape apples on tree. Remove tape and use chart and apples next year.

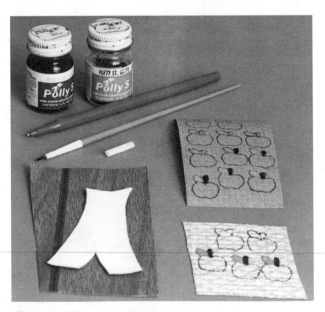

Illustration 273

NOTE

Color or paint leaf and stem of apples. (Allow the paint to dry overnight before putting apples on chart.)

Treetop Pattern
(Trace onto green wallpaper)

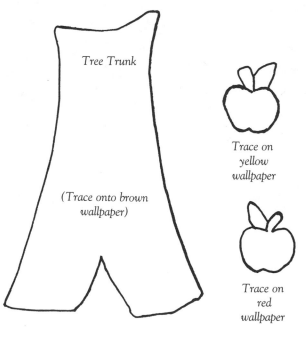

Tree Trunk

(Trace onto brown wallpaper)

Trace on yellow wallpaper

Trace on red wallpaper

Other Ideas for Attendance Chart

DUCKS

Use the pond with a mother duck in it. Add a duckling to the child's pond every Sunday they are there.

SUNFLOWER

Make a large yellow sunflower from yellow wallpaper. Glue a sunflower seed on each child's sunflower for every Sunday they are present.

BIRDS

Use the apple tree. Tape a bird to child's tree every Sunday they are present. Book and Stationery stores have a variety of gummed push-outs including birds.

Waterlily Attendance Chart

Illustration 274

MATERIALS FOR WATERLILY CHART

Scissors, white silk wallpaper, brush, glue, medium green poster board, wallpaper for pond, pink highlighter pen, green highlighter pen, green wallpaper for leaves, black permanent marker, yellow wallpaper for ducks, masking tape and damp cloth.

DIRECTIONS FOR WATERLILY CHART

1. Cut out ponds and glue on green poster board. Place paper towels over ponds and dry under weight.
2. Trace lilies on white wallpaper and draw in lines as shown in illustration 275.
3. Use highlighters to color stems green and base of flowers pink.
4. Cut out leaves. Draw in lines.
5. Next, glue stems of flowers to leaves. Dry and store in box.
6. Make frog, large leaf and two ducklings. Tape to visitors pond.
7. Make cardboard nameplates and have children write in their name.
8. Tape chart to wall.

NOTE

A lily chart can be used in spring or summer. Each Sunday a pupil or visitor is present, they put a lily in their designated pond.

NOTE

Cut 3/8" of masking tape and form into a roll with sticky side out. Flatten and put tape behind each leaf as needed. Flowers are left loose to give a three-dimensional effect. If you prefer a mobile chart, reinforce poster board with corrugated cardboard.

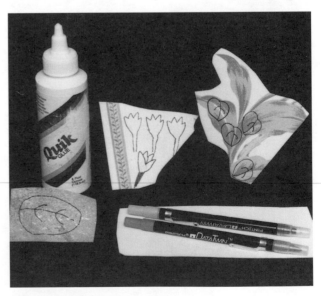

Illustration 275

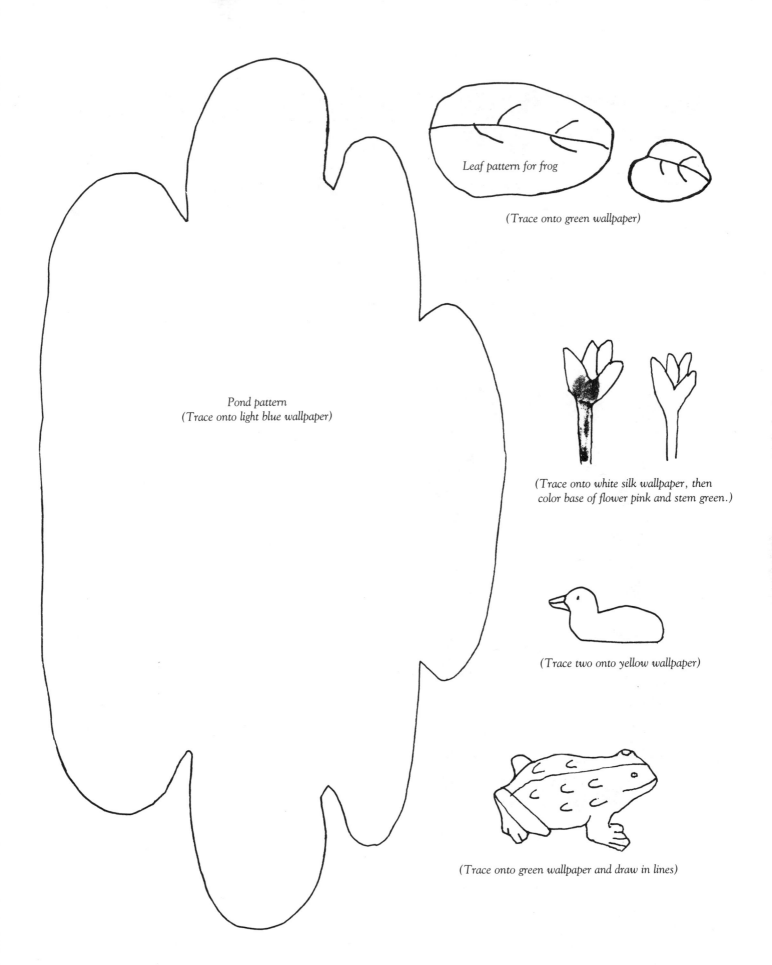

Leaf pattern for frog

(Trace onto green wallpaper)

Pond pattern
(Trace onto light blue wallpaper)

*(Trace onto white silk wallpaper, then
color base of flower pink and stem green.)*

(Trace two onto yellow wallpaper)

(Trace onto green wallpaper and draw in lines)

Gift Bookmark

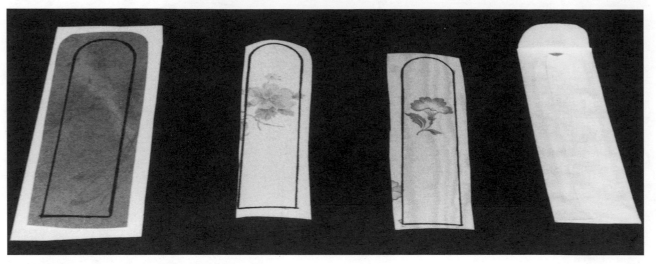

llustration 276

llustration 276

Illustration 277

NOTE

When anyone is given a Bible or book, accompany it with a bookmark. Write recipient's name on the envelope.

MATERIALS FOR GIFT BOOKMARK

Drawing or typing paper, glue, ruler, floral silk wallpaper, and matching plain wallpaper, a damp cloth, scissors, poster board and pinking shears.

DIRECTIONS FOR GIFT BOOKMARK

1. Make pattern A out of plastic. The see-through plastic allows you to center flower. (A cover from a cool Whip container is fine.)
2. Center pattern A over a flower, trace and cut out.
3. Next, cut pattern B from plain wallpaper and glue on poster board.
4. Then, cut around edge of A with pinking shears and glue onto B.
5. Place paper towel over bookmark and dry overnight under weight.
6. Cut out bookmark.

NOTE

Patterns are on page 153.

DIRECTIONS FOR ENVELOPE

1. Draw pattern on drawing paper.
2. Crease on dotted lines.
3. Apply glue between side arrows and glue down sides.
4. Now put glue on bottom tab and glue on top of sides.

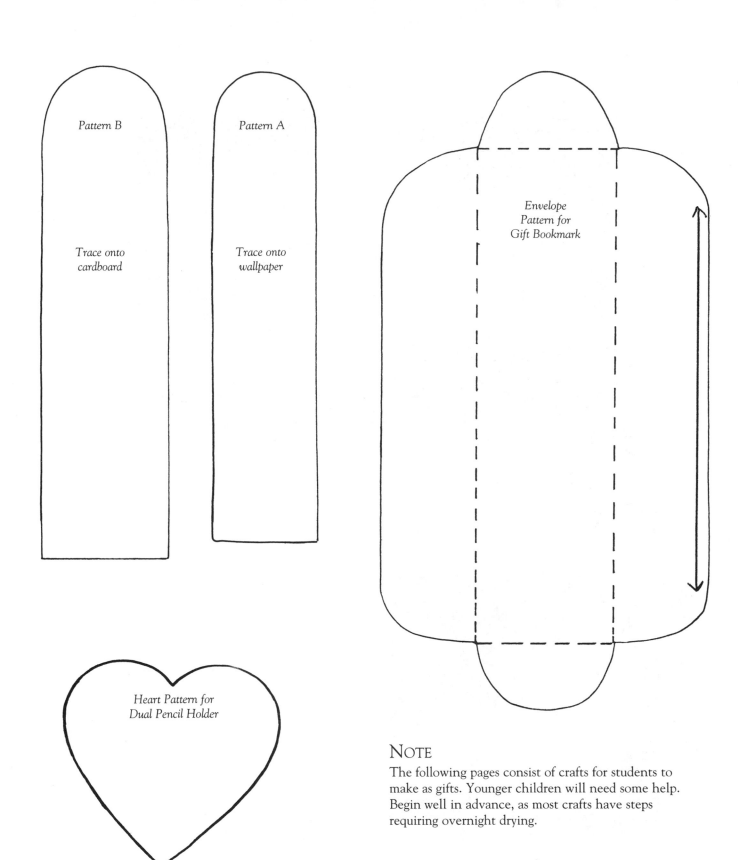

Pattern B

Trace onto
cardboard

Pattern A

Trace onto
wallpaper

Envelope
Pattern for
Gift Bookmark

Heart Pattern for
Dual Pencil Holder

NOTE

The following pages consist of crafts for students to
make as gifts. Younger children will need some help.
Begin well in advance, as most crafts have steps
requiring overnight drying.

Mother's Day Card

Illustration 278

Father's Day Card/Bookmark

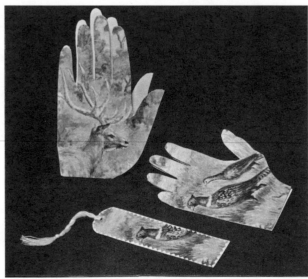

Illustration 279

NOTE
Choose wallpaper with a nature scene for the Father's Day Card and Bookmark.

DIRECTIONS FOR MOTHER'S DAY CARD
1. Cut out a wallpaper flower that is no larger than 4-3/8" by 5".
2. Glue onto fold of poster board.
3. Dry under weight, then cut out.
4. Each child can write his or her own thought inside of card.

DIRECTIONS FOR FATHER'S DAY BOOKMARK
1. Use patterns for Gift Bookmark found on page 153.
2. Trace pattern B onto cardboard.
3. Next, trace pattern A on wallpaper that matches card.
4. Trim with pinking shears. Glue on cardboard and dry under weight.
5. Next, punch a small hole in top of bookmark and tie on a tassel.

DIRECTIONS FOR FATHER'S DAY CARD
1. Place child's left hand (thumb apart and fingers pressed together) on wallpaper and draw around. (See illustration 279.)
2. Now, glue hand on fold of wallpaper and dry under weight.
3. Cut out card. Have child write his or her thought inside of card.

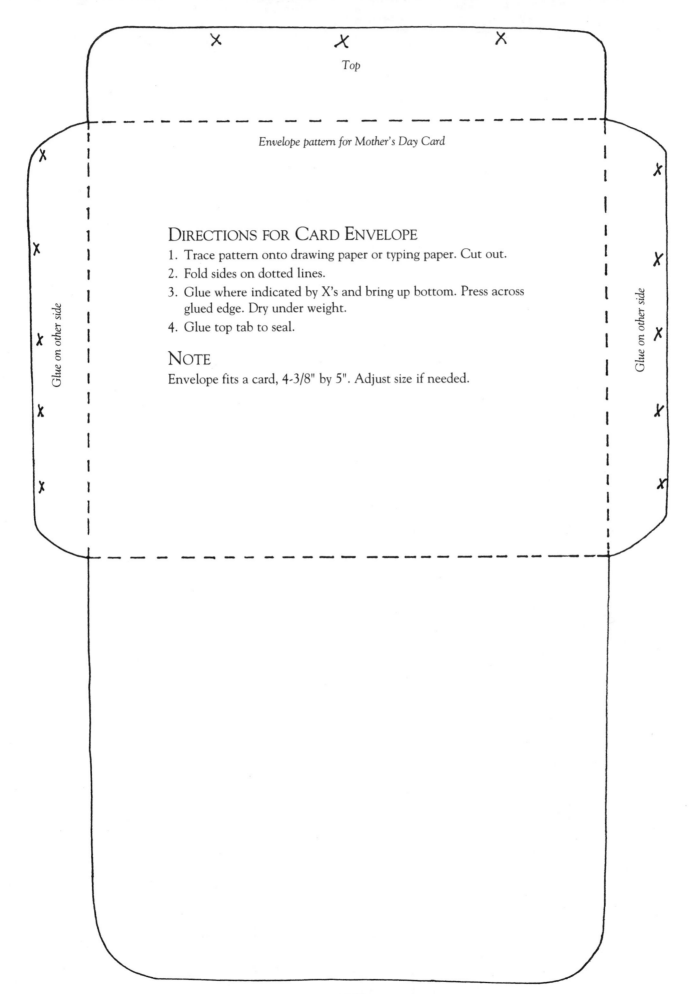

Top

Envelope pattern for Mother's Day Card

Glue on other side

Glue on other side

DIRECTIONS FOR CARD ENVELOPE

1. Trace pattern onto drawing paper or typing paper. Cut out.
2. Fold sides on dotted lines.
3. Glue where indicated by X's and bring up bottom. Press across glued edge. Dry under weight.
4. Glue top tab to seal.

NOTE

Envelope fits a card, 4-3/8" by 5". Adjust size if needed.

Top

Envelope pattern for Father's Day Card

DIRECTIONS FOR CARD ENVELOPE

1. Trace pattern onto drawing paper or typing paper. Cut out.
2. Fold over sides on dotted line.
3. Glue edge of tabs and bring up bottom. Press down on glued edge.
4. Glue top tab to seal.

Silhouette Picture

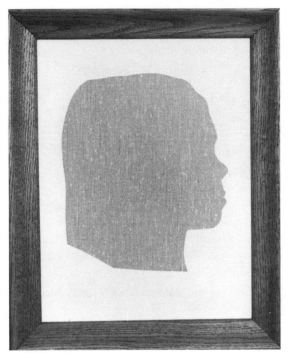

Illustration 280

Plaster Plaque

Illustration 281

MATERIALS FOR SILHOUETTE

Drawing paper, 12" by 16" frame, scissors, carbon paper, damp cloth, thinned glue, brush, ruler, dark wallpaper, foam core and white vinyl wallpaper.

DIRECTIONS FOR MAKING SILHOUETTE

1. Sit model on a chair with left side of head next to wall.
2. Tape paper on wall, level with model's head.
3. Shine a light on the right side of head. Silhouette will appear on drawing paper.
4. Have another person hold light while you trace the silhouette onto drawing paper.

DIRECTIONS FOR SILHOUETTE PICTURE

1. Use carbon paper and trace silhouette onto wrong side of wallpaper. Cut out silhouette.
2. Cut a piece 12" by 16" each of white wallpaper and foam core.
3. Apply glue to the foam core and place wallpaper on top.
4. Press on wallpaper in a sweeping motion, forcing out air pockets. (Use a damp cloth.)
5. Glue silhouette on wallpaper.
6. Dry overnight under weight.
7. Frame. (needs no glass)

DIRECTIONS FOR MOLD

Mix plaster according to instructions and pour into molds. Place a small plastic-coated wire loop on top for a hanger. Leave in mold overnight. Then, remove from mold. Dry for a week before painting.

MATERIALS FOR PLAQUE

Glue, brush, a wallpaper design, acrylic paint, pinking shears and plaster plaque.

DIRECTIONS FOR PLAQUE

1. Paint plaque with a color that matches the walls. Dry overnight.
2. Place plaque over a wallpaper design and trace around.
3. Use pinking shears to trim edge of design to fit top of plaque.
4. Glue design on plaque.

Pen Holder/Desk Calendar

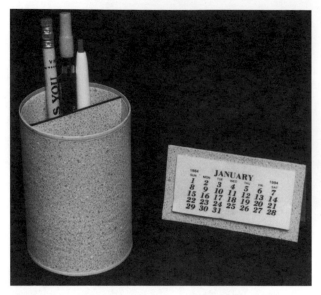

Illustration 282

MATERIALS FOR DESK CALENDAR

Glue, calendar, poster board, wallpaper, ruler, scissors and damp cloth.

DIRECTIONS FOR DESK CALENDAR

1. Cut a piece of poster board 3-1/2" by 4".
2. Score on dotted lines and bend.
3. Cut a piece of wallpaper 2" by 3-1/2" and glue on front.
4. Glue calendar over wallpaper.

MATERIALS FOR PEN HOLDER

Soup can, vinyl wallpaper, scissors, paint, mat board, glue, brush, ruler and damp cloth.

DIRECTIONS FOR PEN HOLDER

1. Wash and remove paper from can.
2. Paint rims of can to coordinate with color of wallpaper. Let dry overnight.
3. Next, cut two pieces of wallpaper 3-11/16" by 8-3/4".
4. Glue onto outside and inside of can.
5. Cut two, 2-1/2" circles. Glue one on inside bottom. (Press down with eraser end of pencil.) Glue other one on outside bottom.
6. Cut a piece of mat board 2-9/16" by 3-3/4". Glue wallpaper on sides.
7. Squeeze can and slide partition down center of can.

NOTE

Ask a framing store for its mat board scraps. They make perfect dividers. Measure precisely for a tight fit and cut with scissors.

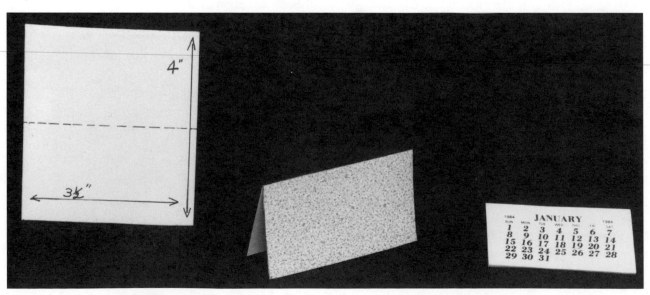

Illustration 283

Dual Pencil Holder

Flower Magnet

Illustration 284

Illustration 285

MATERIALS FOR FLOWER AND BIRD MAGNET

Brush, scissors, Congoleum, glue, permanent marker, wallpaper images, moving eyes, magnetic tape and damp cloth.

DIRECTIONS FOR FLOWER MAGNET

1. Glue a wallpaper image of flower on wrong side of Congoleum. Dry overnight under weight.
2. Cut out image. Now, glue magnet on the back. Dry flat.

DIRECTIONS FOR BIRD MAGNET

1. Follow steps 1 and 2 of Flower Magnet, except use a bird image.
2. Glue a moving eye on bird.
3. Outline image with marker.

MATERIALS FOR DUAL PENCIL HOLDER

Ruler, black mat board, scissors, vinyl wallpaper, glue, damp cloth, half and half carton and red wallpaper for heart.

DIRECTIONS FOR DUAL PENCIL HOLDER

1. Cut down carton to 3-5/8".
2. Cut a piece of mat board 2-11/16" by 2-3/4". Put in bottom of carton. (Trim to fit carton.)
3. Cut a piece of wallpaper 4" by 12". Glue on outside of box. (Snip corners before overlapping wallpaper on bottom and top of box.)
4. Cut another piece of wallpaper 3-3/8" by 11-1/2". Glue inside of box. Dry overnight.
5. Cut a piece of mat board 3-3/8" by 3-3/4". Glue wallpaper on each side. Push down in box diagonally.
6. Use heart pattern to cut out a wallpaper heart. (Heart pattern is on page 153.) Glue on mat board and dry under weight overnight.
7. Cut out heart and glue on front of box. Leave flat until dry.

Bird Magnet

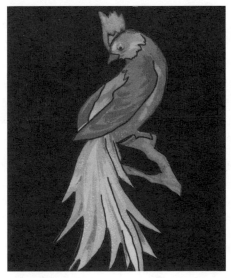

Illustration 286

Miniature Floral Decoration

Illustration 287

MATERIALS FOR FLORAL DECORATION

Scissors, pinking shears, miniature rayon flowers, miniature designed wallpaper, plaster of Paris, glue and mouthwash bottle cap.

DIRECTIONS FOR FLORAL DECORATION

1. Draw pattern on fold of wallpaper. Cut out, then trim edges with pinking shears and glue on cap.
2. Wait five minutes, then press wallpaper down with damp cloth.
3. Next, prepare plaster according to directions. Fill cap to 1/4" from top.
4. Insert flower stems when plaster begins to thicken. (See illustration 287.)

NOTE

A plant is always a welcome gift on Mother's Day. Four to five weeks before Mother's Day, remove baby cacti from a cactus plant and put in a bed of wet sand to root.

Bottle Cap Flowerpot

Illustration 288

MATERIALS FOR BOTTLE CAP FLOWERPOT

Miniature designed wallpaper, glue, mouthwash bottle cap, small cactus and pinking shears.

DIRECTIONS FOR BOTTLE CAP FLOWERPOT

1. Wash bottle cap thoroughly.
2. Draw pattern on fold of wallpaper. (pattern on page 161) Cut out and trim edge with pinking shears.
3. Glue on cap. Wait five minutes and press wallpaper down with damp cloth. Dry overnight.
4. Fill cap 3/4 full with potting soil. Gently press in cactus and spoon in more soil.

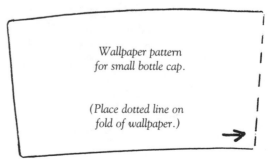

Wallpaper pattern for small bottle cap.

(Place dotted line on fold of wallpaper.)

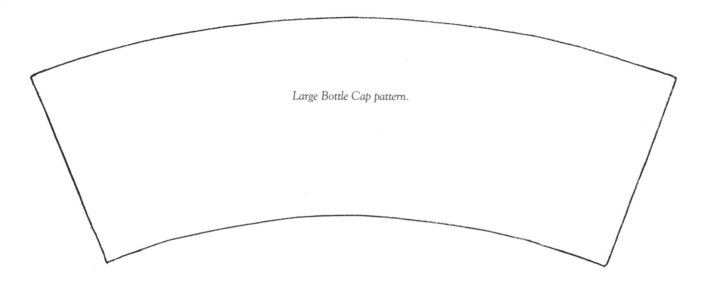

Large Bottle Cap pattern.

Fan

Illustration 289

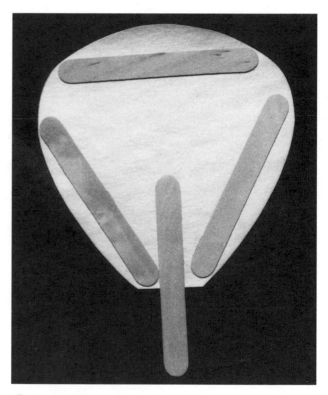

Illustration 290

MATERIALS FOR FAN

Scissors, poster board or any thin cardboard, jumbo craft sticks, thinned glue, vinyl wallpaper with flowers or unusual design and damp cloth.

NOTE

Do not dilute glue for gluing on the craft sticks.

DIRECTIONS FOR FAN

1. Make a cardboard pattern of fan. (found on page 162) Trace on wallpaper.
2. Cut out fan and glue onto cardboard. Dry overnight under weight.
3. Next, cut out cardboard fan.
4. Glue the craft sticks onto back of fan.
5. Weight down overnight.

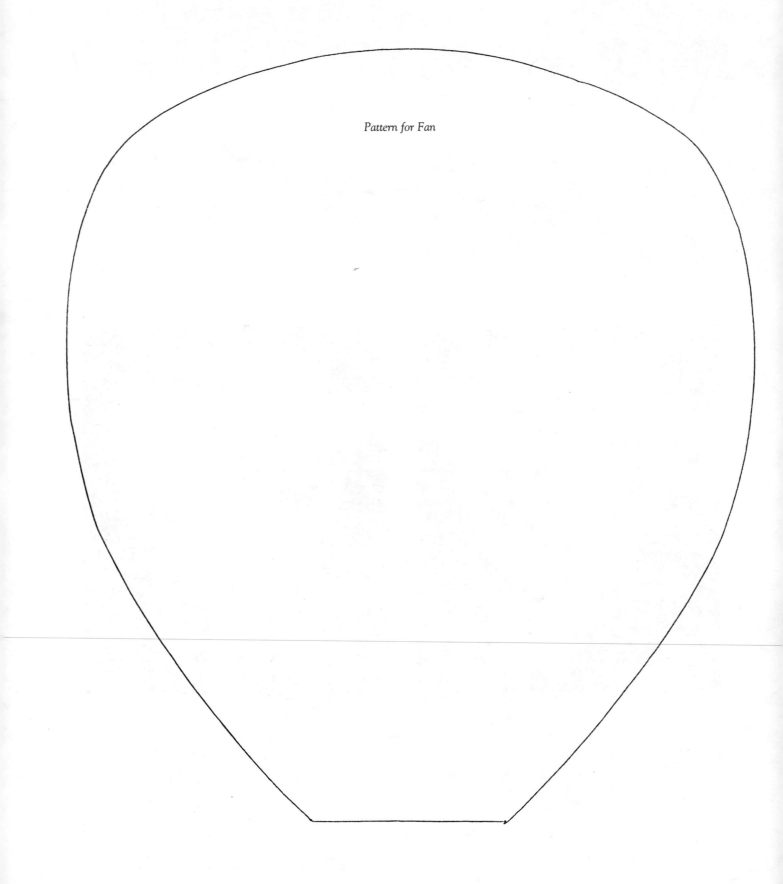

Pattern for Fan

Mom's Wastebasket

Dad's Wastebasket

Illustration 291

Illustration 292

MATERIALS FOR MOM'S WASTEBASKET

Wallpaper paste, large can, white spray paint, flower designed wallpaper, kitchen garbage bag, yardstick, scissors, ruler, 1-1/2" brush, glue and damp cloth.

DIRECTIONS FOR MOM'S WASTEBASKET

1. Wash and dry can thoroughly.

2. Next, spray paint can white.

3. Measure height and circumference of can. (Paste the wallpaper on in three sections, allowing extra paper for overlap.)

4. Paste first piece of wallpaper on can. Wipe out air bubbles with a damp cloth.

5. Continue pasting until can is covered. Press down on surface once more with a damp cloth.

DIRECTIONS FOR DAD'S WASTEBASKET

1. Use directions for Mom's Wastebasket, but use black spray paint. Use wallpaper with nature scenes.

DIRECTIONS FOR WASTEBASKET LINER

1. Use a 13 gallon garbage bag. If it's too big, tape side with transparent tape.

2. Tape (under) a wide hem on top.

3. Fold over top about 3-1/2".

4. Next, cut a strip of matching wallpaper and glue around liner 1" from top edge. (See illustration 291.)

NOTE

Use glue to attach trim onto liner, paste will not adhere. Make an extra liner in case the first one gets damaged or soiled.

Flowerpot Skirt

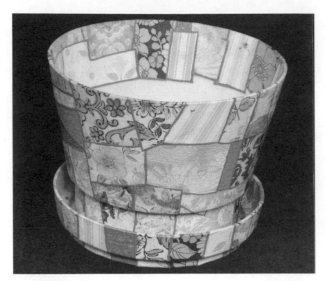

Illustration 293

MATERIALS FOR FLOWERPOT SKIRT

Assorted wallpaper, light blue scale model paint and 5/0 brush, scissors, plastic flowerpot and damp cloth.

DIRECTIONS FOR FLOWERPOT SKIRT

1. Clean a plastic flowerpot.
2. Cut assorted wallpaper pieces in a crazy quilt fashion.
3. Glue pieces over edges first, slightly overlapping each other.
4. Dry overnight.
5. Outline with scale model paint.
6. Dry. Place flowerpot in skirt.

Jewelry Tray

Illustration 294

MATERIALS FOR JEWELRY TRAY

Gluing brush, size 5/0 brush for outlining, glue, blue scale model paint, meat tray, assorted wallpaper, scissors and damp cloth.

DIRECTIONS FOR JEWELRY TRAY

1. Cut assorted wallpaper pieces in a crazy quilt fashion.
2. Glue pieces over edges first, slightly overlapping each other.
3. Dry overnight.
4. Outline with scale model paint.
5. Remove jewelry and put in tray while doing dishes.

NOTE

Do not use vinyl wallpaper.

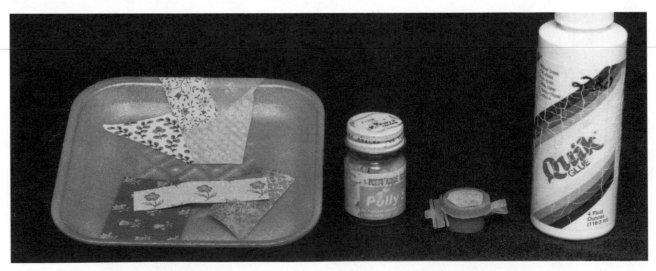

Illustration 295

Christmas Decorations

Christmas Decorations

Photo by Mark Lynch

Photo Tree Ornament

Illustration 296

Illustration 297

MATERIALS FOR PHOTO ORNAMENT

Thin cardboard, Christmas-like wallpaper, toothpick, glitter, scissors, curling ribbon, glue, photo and a small brush.

NOTE

Use undiluted glue when gluing on glitter.
It dries faster.

DIRECTIONS FOR PHOTO ORNAMENT

1. Trace one each of pattern A on thin cardboard and wallpaper.
2. Glue the wallpaper circle onto the cardboard one.
3. Make a plastic pattern B. Then, center over photo and cut out.
4. Glue photo on wallpaper.
5. Circle photo with glue. (Use a toothpick and undiluted glue.)
6. Shake glitter on glue. Let dry.
7. Shake off loose glitter and tie on ribbon hanger.

Dove Ornament

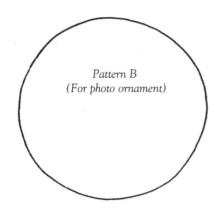

Pattern B
(For photo ornament)

Pattern
for
Dove Ornament

Illustration 299

MATERIALS FOR DOVE ORNAMENT

Glue, thin cardboard, tiny moving eyes, white wallpaper, invisible thread, scissors and white glitter.

DIRECTIONS FOR DOVE ORNAMENT

1. Make a plastic pattern and cut one each of cardboard and wallpaper.
2. Glue wallpaper dove on the cardboard dove. Glue on eye.
3. Apply glue on surface of dove and shake on glitter.
4. When dry, attach hanger with a needle and invisible thread.

Styrofoam Ornament

Illustration 298

MATERIALS FOR STYROFOAM ORNAMENT

Shiny wallpaper, Styrofoam balls, undiluted glue, hanger pins, small paper punch, curling ribbon, damp cloth and toothpick.

DIRECTIONS FOR STYROFOAM ORNAMENT

1. Punch out circles of wallpaper and glue on balls. (use toothpick) Press on with a damp cloth.
2. Attach hanger pin and ribbon.

Christmas Chain

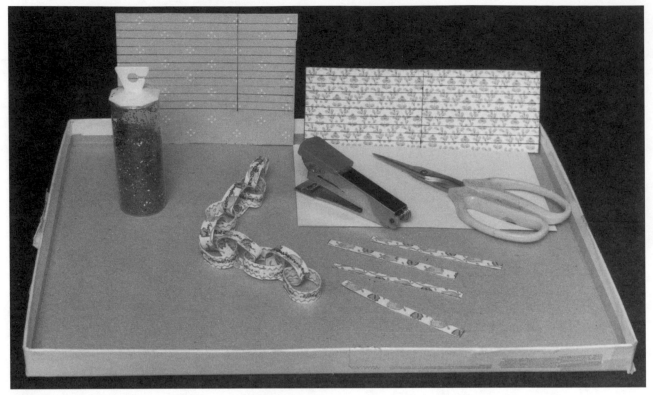

Illustration 300

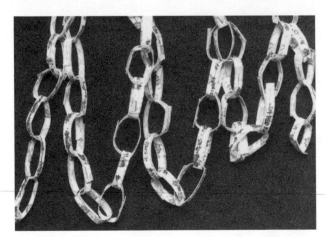

Illustration 301

NOTE
Staple the links before putting on the glitter so it doesn't plug up the stapler.

MATERIALS FOR CHRISTMAS CHAIN
Glitter, Christmas-like wallpaper, stapler, wallpaper paste, scissors, damp cloth, undiluted glue and a box cover in which to shake glitter onto links.

DIRECTIONS FOR CHRISTMAS CHAIN
1. Paste two sheets of wallpaper, back-to-back.
2. Press out air bubbles with damp cloth or wallpaper brush.
3. Cover with paper towels and dry overnight under weight.
4. Mark your wallpaper into strips 1/4" by 3-5/8". (See illustration 300.)
5. Cut out strips.
6. Next, staple chain. (Staple one link, interlock another and staple and so on until finished.)
7. Now, shake on the glitter. This works faster if one person puts a tiny stream of glue in the center of links while someone else shakes the glitter on the glue. (Undiluted glue dries fast and won't run.)
8. Do this in a box cut down to 2" or a box cover. When finished, put excess glitter back in container.
9. Optional: It's not necessary to use glitter with bright wallpaper.

Glitter Balls

MATERIALS FOR GLITTER BALLS

Hanger pins, undiluted glue, brush, glitter, soft wallpaper with miniature design, curling ribbon, Styrofoam balls and a damp cloth.

DIRECTIONS FOR GLITTER BALLS

1. Glue wallpaper on in strips. To learn the technique of tearing the wallpaper, refer to page 29.
2. Overlap strips just enough to cover Styrofoam. When done, press ball with damp cloth. Let dry.
3. Attach hanger. Then, glaze ball with thinned glue. Hang to dry.
4. Now, trickle thin lines of glue around ball. Immediately shake on glitter and hang to dry.
5. Tie on hanger ribbon.

NOTE

Wipe your hands often with a damp cloth because sticky fingers pull the strips off. Also, do not use vinyl wallpaper for this type of craft.

Illustration 302

Illustration 303

Christmas Cards

Illustration 304

MATERIALS FOR CARDS

Glue, curling ribbon, brush, paper punch, bright wallpaper, Christmas cards, glue, thin cardboard, glitter, scissors and toothpick.

DIRECTIONS FOR CHRISTMAS CARDS

1. Cut out scene from used Christmas cards that can be enhanced by glitter. (See illustration 304.)
2. Cut out a pattern 2-1/2" by 2" or a 2" circle. Cut one each of wallpaper and thin cardboard.
3. Glue wallpaper onto cardboard.
4. Next, cut out scene 3/8" smaller than wallpaper. Glue in center of wallpaper and dry under weight.
5. Use toothpick to make lines of glue where you want the glitter.
6. Shake glitter over glue. Do the same for border and dry overnight.
7. Punch out holes and tie ribbon.

Christmas Centerpiece

MATERIALS FOR CENTERPIECE

Plaster of Paris, pine cone, bake cup container, beads, ribbon, glue, glitter and brush.

DIRECTIONS FOR CENTERPIECE

1. Cut a bake cup container down to 1-1/2".
2. Mix plaster of Paris according to directions. Put stem of cone in plaster before it sets.
3. Thread beads on a ribbon. Then, string it around cone.
4. Apply glue to tips of cone and shake on white glitter. Store in a plastic bag.

Illustration 305

Canister Decoration

Illustration 306

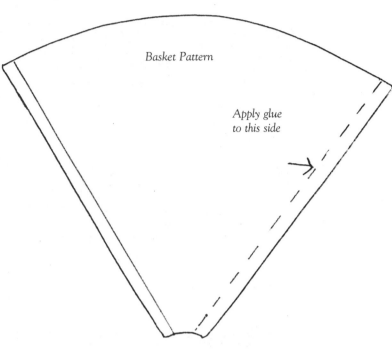

Basket Pattern

Apply glue
to this side

MATERIALS FOR
CANISTER DECORATION

Film canister, miniature designed wallpaper, red glitter, glue, ribbon and paper punch.

DIRECTIONS FOR
CANISTER DECORATION

1. Cut a piece of wallpaper 1-3/4" by 4-1/2" and glue on canister.

2. Punch a hole 3/8" from the top of canister. Thread a 7-3/4" long ribbon through outside of hole and tie a double knot on end, inside.

3. Do same on opposite side.

4. Trickle a line of glue around top and bottom of canister. Shake glitter over glue. Dry well.

Candy Cane Basket

MATERIALS FOR CANDY CANE BASKET

Red wallpaper, ribbon, glue, scissors, brush and white wallpaper.

DIRECTIONS FOR CANDY CANE BASKET

1. Cut basket from red wallpaper.
2. Apply glue where indicated and roll into cone. Press together until glue sets.
3. Bend a 5-1/2" long ribbon in half.
4. Glue ends on outside of cone.
5. Glue a strip of white wallpaper around top of basket, over ribbon.
6. Place candy cane in basket.

Illustration 307

Christmas Wreath

Illustration 308

Illustration 309

NOTE
Use predominating colors of red and green.

MATERIALS FOR CHRISTMAS WREATH
Optional: artificial sprig of mistletoe, Congoleum, a piece of red cloth 45" long, by 4-3/4" wide to make bow, scissors, glue, brush, assorted wallpaper, ruler, 6" of plastic coated wire, yardstick and a damp cloth.

DIRECTIONS FOR CHRISTMAS WREATH
1. First make a pattern by drawing an 11-1/2" circle. (Use bowl or a pie tin.) Then, center another circle 7-1/4" on the inside of other circle.
2. Trace pattern onto Congoleum.
3. Cut out, then glue on wallpaper pieces in crazy quilt fashion. Be sure to overlap edges. Let dry.
4. Now, sew a ribbon like a sash.
5. Punch two holes 1/2" apart in the top center of wreath.
6. Sew mistletoe to bow.
7. Next, thread wire through back of bow, twist and push ends in the holes of wreath. Twist wire tight.
8. Then, make a loop for hanger on end of wire. Trim off excess wire from the other end of wire.
9. Hang wreath in doorway or window.

Candy Ornament

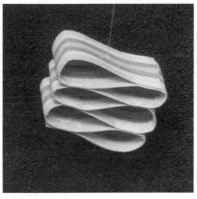

Illustration 310

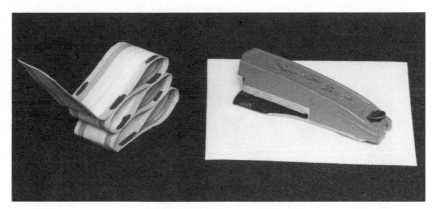

Illustration 312

MATERIALS FOR CANDY ORNAMENT

Ruler, striped wallpaper, brush, stapler, scissors, invisible thread, wallpaper paste and damp cloth.

DIRECTIONS FOR CANDY ORNAMENT

1. Cut two pieces of striped wallpaper 17" long and 12" wide.
2. Paste them back-to-back and dry under weight. (enough for several)
3. Cut off a strip 1-1/2" by 17".
4. Fold strip, accordian fashion, every two inches. Staple each end to above fold. (See photo indicating where by a black mark.)
5. Make a hanger out of invisible thread. (Thread a 2-1/2" loop through top center of candy ornament.)

Christmas Tree Box

Illustration 311

MATERIALS FOR CHRISTMAS TREE BOX

Glue, scissors, wooden box 18" by 18" and 16" high, assorted wallpaper and damp cloth.

DIRECTIONS FOR CHRISTMAS TREE BOX

1. Make a wooden box out of scrap material using above measurements.
2. Tape over cracks and holes with masking tape.
3. Glue on assorted wallpaper in a crazy quilt fashion. (Overlap pieces on edges.)
4. Press down each piece with damp cloth as you go.

NOTE

The box accommodates a small tree. Tip upside down and place a small red cloth on it.

Christmas Notes

Illustration 313

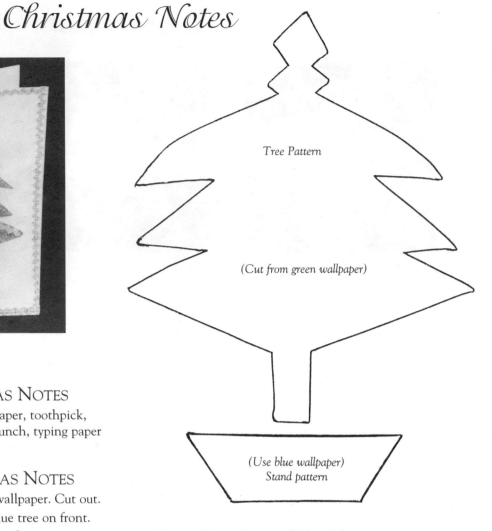

Tree Pattern

(Cut from green wallpaper)

(Use blue wallpaper)
Stand pattern

MATERIALS FOR CHRISTMAS NOTES

Pinking shears, medium green wallpaper, toothpick, damp cloth, gold wallpaper, paper punch, typing paper and glue.

DIRECTIONS FOR CHRISTMAS NOTES

1. Trace the tree pattern on green wallpaper. Cut out.
2. Fold a typing sheet in fourths. Glue tree on front.
3. Cut 3/8" strips of gold wallpaper with pinking shears.
4. Glue strips around edge of paper and across tree. (See illustration 313.)
5. Use a paper punch to punch out wallpaper circles. Apply glue on circles and press on with a toothpick.

6. Use an old envelope 4-1/2" by 6" for pattern to make envelope from drawing paper.

Gift Box Ornament

DIRECTIONS FOR GIFT BOX ORNAMENT

1. Use small jewelry-type box.
2. Glue wallpaper on cover of box.
3. Tie a ribbon around box. Glue a small star with glitter onto box.
4. Attach invisible thread to ribbon for hanger.

Illustration 314

Below are geometic patterns for page 20

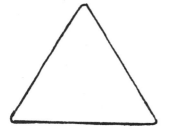 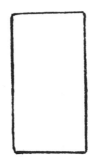 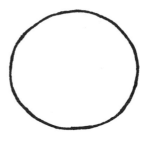

Below are patterns for Small Frames on page 5

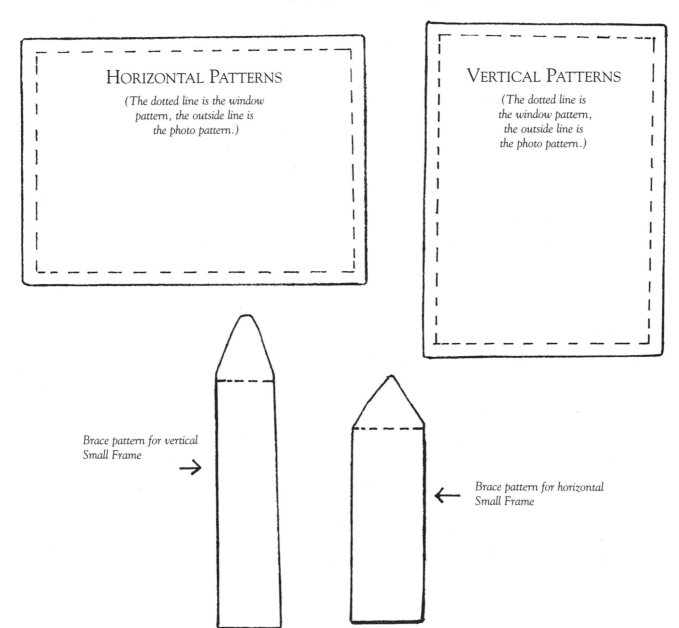

HORIZONTAL PATTERNS

(The dotted line is the window pattern, the outside line is the photo pattern.)

VERTICAL PATTERNS

(The dotted line is the window pattern, the outside line is the photo pattern.)

Brace pattern for vertical Small Frame →

← *Brace pattern for horizontal Small Frame*

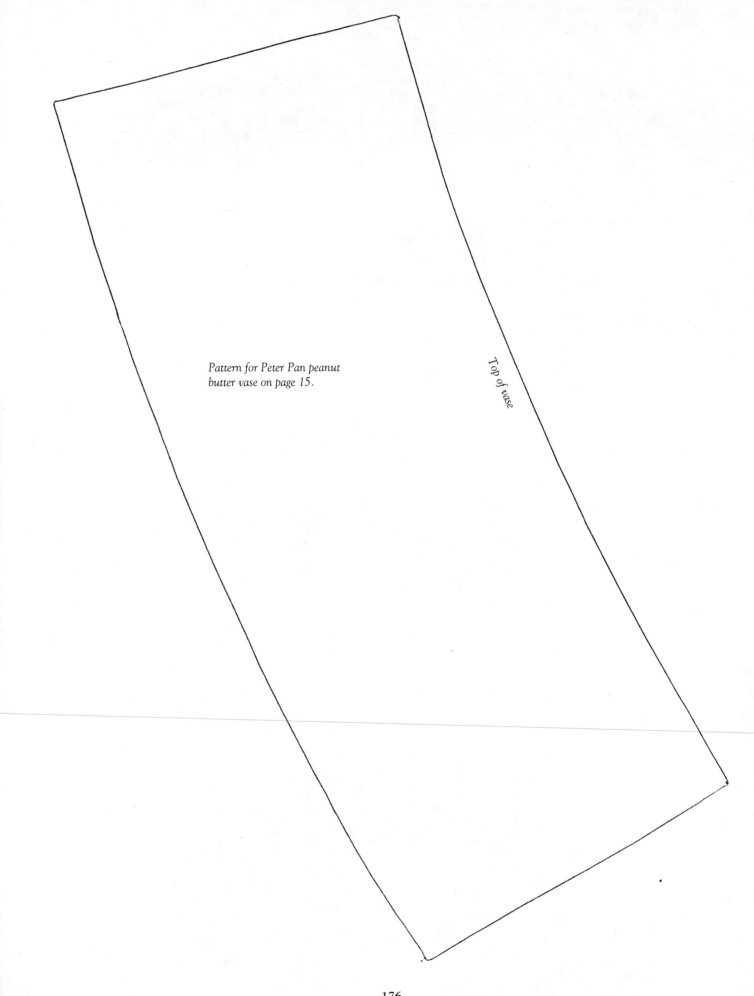

Pattern for Peter Pan peanut
butter vase on page 15.

Top of vase

Ordered by:

Name

Address

City   State   Zip

Area Code   Telephone Number

Qty.	Book No.	Crafty Recycling	Unit Price	Total Price
	2002	Softcover	$12.95	
	2003	Hardcover	$18.00	

Merchandise Total

Shipping & Handling

6-1/2% Sales Tax (84¢ each softcover book) ($1.17 each hardcover book)
(MN residents only)

(Please add $2.50 for Shipping, $1.00 for each additional book.)   Total Price

Send Check or Money Order to:

Tassel Press
P.O. Box 6342
Minneapolis, MN 55406

Ordered by:

Name

Address

City   State   Zip

Area Code   Telephone Number

Qty.	Book No.	Crafty Recycling	Unit Price	Total Price
	2002	Softcover	$12.95	
	2003	Hardcover	$18.00	

Merchandise Total

Shipping & Handling

6-1/2% Sales Tax (84¢ each softcover book) ($1.17 each hardcover book)
(MN residents only)

(Please add $2.50 for Shipping, $1.00 for each additional book.)   Total Price

Send Check or Money Order to:

Tassel Press
P.O. Box 6342
Minneapolis, MN 55406